A Short History of Drunkenness

A Short History of Drunkenness

HOW, WHY, WHERE, AND WHEN HUMANKIND
HAS GOTTEN MERRY FROM THE STONE AGE
TO THE PRESENT

MARK FORSYTH

THREE RIVERS PRESS • NEW YORK

Originally published in Great Britain by Viking, an imprint
of Penguin Random House UK, London, in 2017.

Three Rivers Press and the Tugboat design are registered
trademarks of Penguin Random House LLC.

Grateful acknowledgment is made to United Agents LLP on
behalf of the Executors of the Estate of Jocelyn Herbert,
M. T. Perkins and Polly M. V. R. Perkins for permission to quote from
A. P. Herbert's "Some Aspects of Hyperhydrophilia,"
in Cyril Ray (ed.), *The Compleat Imbiber,* Vol. 1.

Library of Congress Cataloging-in-Publication Data is available

ISBN 978-0-525-57537-5
Ebook ISBN 978-0-525-57538-2

Printed in the United States of America

Book design by Jouve UK, Milton Keynes
Illustrations by Mark Forsyth
Jacket design and illustration by Zak Tebbal

10 9 8 7 6 5 4 3

Contents

CONTENTS

Introduction

I'm afraid that I don't really know what drunkenness is. That may seem an odd confession for a fellow who's about to write a history of drunkenness, but, to be honest, if authors were to let a trifling thing like ignorance stop them from writing, the bookshops would be empty. Anyway, I do have some idea. I have been conducting extensive empirical investigations on drunkenness ever since the tender age of fourteen. In many ways, I like to think of myself as being a sort of latter-day St. Augustine who asked, "What then is time? If no one asks me, I know what it is. If I wish to explain it to him who asks, I do not know." Substitute the word *drunkenness* for *time* and you pretty much have my saintly position.

I'm aware of some basic medical facts. A couple of gin and tonics will impair your reflexes; a dozen or so will reacquaint you with your lunch and make it difficult to stand up, and an uncertain number, which I am unwilling to investigate, will kill you. But that's not what we know (in an Augustinian way) drunkenness is. Certainly, if an alien knocked on my door and asked why people across this peculiar planet keep drinking alcohol, I wouldn't answer, "Oh, that's just to impair our reflexes. It's basically to stop us getting too good at Ping-Pong."

There's another canard which is usually trotted out at

this point, that alcohol lowers your inhibitions. Nothing could be further from the truth. I do all sorts of things when I'm squiffy that I never *wanted* to do when sober. I can talk for hours to people that, sober, I would consider tedious. I recall once leaning out of the window of a flat in Camden Town waving a crucifix about and telling passersby to repent. This isn't something that I long to do when sober but just don't have the nerve for.

Anyway, some of alcohol's effects are not caused by alcohol. It's terribly easy to hand out nonalcoholic beer without telling people that it contains no alcohol. You then watch them drink and take notes. Sociologists do this all the time, and the results are consistent and conclusive. First, you can't trust a sociologist at the bar; they must be watched like hawks. Second, if you come from a culture where alcohol is meant to make you aggressive, you get aggressive. If you come from a culture where it's meant to make you religious, you become religious. You can even change this from drinking session to drinking session. If the devious sociologist announces that they're investigating liquor and libido, everyone gets libidinous; if they say it's about song, everyone suddenly bursts out singing.

People even alter their behavior depending on what species of booze they think they're imbibing. Even though the active ingredient—ethanol—is identical, people will alter their behavior depending on the origins and cultural associations of the tipple in question. English people are very likely to get aggressive after a few pints of lager, but give them wine—which is associated with poshness and

France—and they will become demure, urbane and, in serious cases, sprout a beret. There's a reason we have lager-louts but not vermouth-vandals or Campari-contrarians.

Some people get very angry when you tell them this. They insist that alcohol causes whatever it is that they don't like—let's say violence. If you point out that cultures where alcohol is banned are still violent, they harrumph. If I point out, which I can, that I drink an awful lot more than most, but that I haven't hit anyone since the age of about eight (before intoxicating liquors had ever touched my pacific lips), they say, "Well, yes, but what about other people?" It's always other people, damn them—other people are hell. But most people are able to drink all evening at a nice dinner party without once stabbing the guest on their right.

And, in the unlikely event that you were suddenly transported to another time and place, an Ancient Egyptian would probably be very surprised that you weren't drinking to receive a vision of the lion-headed goddess Hathor—I thought *everyone* did that. And a Neolithic shaman would wonder why you weren't communicating with the ancestors. A Suri of Ethiopia would probably ask why you hadn't started work yet. That's what Suri people do when they drink; as the saying goes, "Where there is no beer, there is no work." Just as an incidental technical point, this is called transitional drinking: drinking to mark the transition from one bit of the day to the other. In England we drink because we've finished working, the Suri drink because they've started.

To put this all another way, when Margaret Thatcher

died she was not buried with all her wineglasses and a corner-shop's worth of booze. We think this normal. In fact, we'd think it odd if she had been. But we are the odd ones, we're the weirdos, we're the eccentrics. For most of known human history political leaders have been buried with all things needful for a good postmortem piss-up. That goes all the way back to King Midas, to Proto-Dynastic Egypt, to the shamans of Ancient China and, of bloody course, to the Vikings. Even those who have long stopped breathing like to get trolleyed now and then—just ask the Tiriki tribe of Kenya, who go and pour beer onto their ancestors' graves just in case.

Drunkenness is near universal. Almost every culture in the world has booze. The only ones that weren't too keen—North America and Australia—have been colonized by those who were. And at every time and in every place, drunkenness is a different thing. It's a celebration, a ritual, an excuse to hit people, a way of making decisions or ratifying contracts, and a thousand other peculiar practices. When the Ancient Persians had a big political decision to make they would debate the matter twice: once drunk, and once sober. If they came to the same conclusion both times, they acted.

That is what this book is about. It's not about alcohol per se, it's about drunkenness: its pitfalls and its gods. From Ninkasi, the Sumerian goddess of beer, to the 400 drunken rabbits of Mexico.

A couple of points should be made before we set off. First, this is a *short* history. A complete history of drunkenness would be a complete history of humanity and require much too much paper. Instead, I have decided to pick certain points in history to see how people went about getting sozzled. What was it actually like in a Wild West saloon, or a medieval English alehouse, or a Greek symposium? When an Ancient Egyptian girl wanted to go out on the lash what exactly did she do? Of course, each evening is different, but it's possible to get a good, if hazy, notion.

History books like to tell us that so-and-so was drunk, but they don't explain the minutiae of drinking. Where was it done? With whom? At what time of day? Drinking has always been surrounded by rules, but they rarely get written down. In present-day Britain, for example, though there is no law in place, absolutely everybody knows that you must not drink before noon, except, for some reason, in airports and at cricket matches.

But in the middle of the rules is unruly drunkenness. The anarchist at the cocktail party. She (I think it's a she, deities of drink usually are) is the one I want to watch. Ideally, I'd like to arrest her and take her mugshot, but I'm not sure it's possible. At least then, when that curious alien asked me what drunkenness was, I would have something to show.

CHAPTER I

EVOLUTION

We must recall that Nature's laws
Are generally sound,
And everywhere, for some good cause,
Some alcohol is found.
There's alcohol in plant and tree,
It must be Nature's plan
That there should be, in fair degree,
Some alcohol in Man.

A. P. Herbert (1956)

Before we were human, we were drinkers. Alcohol occurs naturally and always has. When life began four-billion-and-something years ago there were single-cell microbes happily swimming around in the primordial broth eating simple sugars and excreting ethanol and carbon dioxide. Essentially they were pissing beer.

Fortunately, life progressed and we got trees and fruit, and fruit, if left to rot, quite naturally ferments.

Fermentation produces sugar and alcohol, and fruit flies seek it out and gobble it up. It is not known whether fruit flies get drunk in any way that we humans might understand. They are, alas, incapable of talking, or singing songs, or driving cars. All we know for sure is that if a male fruit fly has his romantic advances spurned by a cruel and disdainful female fruit fly, he ups his alcohol consumption dramatically.

Unfortunately for animals, alcohol doesn't occur naturally in large enough quantities to allow for a proper party. Well, sometimes it does. There's an island off Panama where the mantled howler monkey can feast happily on the fallen fruit of the astrocaryum palm (4.5 percent ABV). They get boisterous and noisy, and then they get sleepy and stumbly, and then sometimes they fall out of trees and injure themselves. If you adjust their alcohol intake for bodyweight, they can get through the equivalent of two bottles of wine in thirty minutes. But they are a rarity. For most animals there's just not enough booze to go around, unless a kindly scientist catches you, puts you in laboratory conditions and plies you with the stuff.

Drunk animals are rather fun, and one can't help but suspect that the scientists who spend their time carefully setting up experiments to see how alcohol affects the brains and behavior of our quadruped cousins are quietly giggling the entire time. What happens when you give a rat a tipple, or indeed an unlimited supply of alcohol? What happens if you give a whole colony of rats an open bar?

Actually, they're rather civilized. Though not for the

first few days. For the first few days they go a bit crazy, but then most of them settle down to two drinks a day: one just before feeding (which the scientists refer to as the cocktail hour) and one just before bedtime (the nightcap). Every three or four days there's a spike in alcohol consumption as all the rats get together for little rat parties. It all sounds rather idyllic, and you'd be forgiven for wishing that you had been born a rat. But you must remember two things: first, not all rats are lucky enough to be experimented upon in a laboratory; second, there is a dark side to murine drunkenness. Rat colonies usually have one dominant male, the King Rat. The King Rat is a teetotaler. Alcohol consumption is highest among the males with the lowest social status. They drink to calm their nerves, they drink to forget their worries, they drink, it seems, because they're failures.

And that's one of the biggest problems with trying to study animal boozing. It's so stressful to be locked up and prodded and poked that the poor brute will take any intoxicant you give it. And, to be fair, it would work the other way round. If I were captured by a pack of orangutans who dragged me off to the forest canopy of Borneo and plied me with dry martinis, I'd probably drink them, not least because I'm afraid of heights.

So scientists have to find subtle ways of giving animals drinks without alarming them. This is particularly true of elephants, as you don't want to alarm a drunk elephant under any circumstances. They turn violent. There was a case in India in 1985 when a herd of elephants managed to break into a distillery, and it didn't turn out at all well.

There were 150 of them and they all got fighting drunk and went on something of a rampage. They ripped down seven concrete buildings and trampled five people to death. Frankly, one drunken elephant is one too many; 150 is properly problematic.

You can do these things in a rather more controlled way in a wildlife park. Load a couple of barrels of beer onto the back of a pickup truck, drive to somewhere near the elephants, take the lids off and let them have a sip. There's usually a bit of jostling and the big bull elephants take most of it. But you can then observe them stumbling around and falling asleep and it's all rather amusing. Even this, though, can go wrong. One scientist who allowed a dominant bull to get a bit too pissed found himself having to break up a fight between a soused elephant and a rhino. Usually, elephants don't attack rhinos, but the beer makes them quarrelsome.

It's a lot safer to stick to ants. There used to be a theory that ants had passwords. Ants live in colonies and they don't let in strange ants from other colonies. This raises the question of how they know who's who. The password theory was a bit odd, but it was reasonably popular among whimsical Victorian naturalists until it was thoroughly debunked by Sir John Lubbock, 1st Baron Avebury, following some experiments in the 1870s:

> It has been suggested that the Ants of each nest have some sign or password by which they recognize one another. To test this I made some insensible. First I tried chloroform, but this was fatal to them; and . . . I did not

consider the test satisfactory. I decided therefore to intoxicate them. This was less easy than I had expected. None of my Ants would voluntarily degrade themselves by getting drunk. However, I got over the difficulty by putting them into whisky for a few moments. I took fifty specimens, twenty-five from one nest and twenty-five from another, made them dead drunk, marked each with a spot of paint, and put them on a table close to where other Ants from one of the nests were feeding. The table was surrounded as usual with a moat of water to prevent them from straying. The Ants which were feeding soon noticed those which I had made drunk. They seemed quite astonished to find their comrades in such a disgraceful condition, and as much at a loss to know what to do with their drunkards as we are. After a while, however, to cut my story short, they carried them all away; the strangers they took to the edge of the moat and dropped into the water, while they bore their friends home into the nest, where by degrees they slept off the effects of the spirit. Thus it is evident that they know their friends even when incapable of giving any sign or password.

This may sound silly and whimsical, but the continuities between human drunkenness and animal drunkenness, the way that the furry mirror the smooth, actually influenced the greatest advance of Victorian biology. Charles Darwin thought that drunken apes were funny. They are. But he also thought that they were significant. He was fascinated to hear about how you catch a baboon:

The natives of north-eastern Africa catch the wild baboons by exposing vessels with strong beer, by which they are made drunk. [A German zoologist] has seen some of these animals, which he kept in confinement, in this state; and he gives a laughable account of their behaviour and strange grimaces. On the following morning they were very cross and dismal; they held their aching heads with both hands and wore a most pitiable expression: when beer or wine was offered them, they turned away with disgust, but relished the juice of lemons. An American monkey, an Ateles, after getting drunk on brandy, would never touch it again, and thus was wiser than many men. These trifling facts prove how similar the nerves of taste must be in monkeys and man.

If, Darwin thought, man and monkey both react the same way to hangovers, they must be related. This wasn't his only proof, but it was a start in proving that bishops were primates.

It is also a forerunner of a much more recent theory of furry parentage.

The Drunken Monkey Hypothesis

Humans are designed to drink. We're really damned good at it. Better than any other mammal, except maybe the Malaysian tree shrew. Never get into a drinking contest with a Malaysian tree shrew; or, if you do, don't let them insist that you adjust for bodyweight. They can take nine glasses of wine and be none the worse for it. That's because they've evolved to survive on fermented palm nectar. For millions of years evolution has been naturally selecting the best shrew drinkers in Malaysia and now they're champions.

But we are the same. We evolved to drink. Ten million years ago our ancestors came down from the trees. Why they did this is not entirely clear, but it may well be that they were after the lovely overripe fruit that you find on the forest floor. That fruit has more sugar in it and more alcohol. So we developed noses that could smell the alcohol at a distance. The alcohol was a marker that could lead us to the sugar.

This leads to what is known to scientists as the aperitif effect. The taste of alcohol, the smell of alcohol, makes us want to feed. This is, if you think about it, a little odd. Alcohol contains lots of calories: why would consuming some calories make you want to consume more?

People will tell you that a little G&T stimulates the digestive system, but that isn't true. You can administer the alcohol intravenously and you get the same effect. Nor is it that drunk dieters simply lose their self-control. Alcohol triggers a particular neuron* in the brain that makes you terribly, terribly hungry. It's the same neuron that gets triggered when you are actually, really, truly starving. This makes perfect sense for a chap ten million years ago. You're rambling around on the forest floor, feeling perhaps a tad nostalgic for the treetops, when you smell

---

* The hypothalamic AgRP neuron, to be precise. Not that I have any idea what that is.

something lovely: overripe fruit. You follow the scent and find a great big melon or whatnot. It's more than you can comfortably eat at one sitting, but you should go ahead anyway. You can store all those calories as fat and burn them later. So now you get a feedback system: each bite gives you some alcohol, which goes to your brain and makes you hungrier and hungrier, so you eat more and that makes you want to eat more and as a result, 500,000 generations later, your descendant, staggering home from the pub, decides that they'd kill for a kebab.

But back to ten million years ago. Alcohol has led us to our food, alcohol has made us want to eat our food, but now we need to process the alcohol; otherwise we'll just become food for somebody else. It's hard enough to fight off a prehistoric predator when you're sober, but trying to punch a saber-toothed tiger when you're five sheets to the wind is a nightmare.

So now that we'd acquired the taste, we needed—evolutionarily—to develop a coping mechanism. There is one quite precise genetic mutation that occurred ten million years ago that makes us process alcohol nearly as well as a Malaysian shrew. It's to do with the production of a particular enzyme* that we started to produce. Humans (or the ancestors of humans) were suddenly able to drink all the other apes under the table. For a modern human, 10 percent of the enzyme machinery in your liver is devoted to converting alcohol into energy.

---

* Ethanol-active Class IV alcohol dehydrogenases (ADH4), to be precise. Not that I have the foggiest what they are.

But there is one final development that's the most important one to us: how we drink. Humans drink socially. We offer alcohol around to our group. We get all warm and fuzzy and tell people that they're our best friends and we love them and all that other guff. The most interesting part of the Drunken Monkey Hypothesis is that this is all evolutionary programming. We enjoy alcohol because it's our reward for eating all those calories. We share it with our group because it makes sense for apes to feed their families and their pack. We drink together because it provides protection from predators. One drunk human is prey, twenty drunk humans will make the hungriest saber-toothed tiger think twice.

Now that last bit is the most speculative part of the theory, but it's pretty convincing. We humans are champion boozehounds and the Drunken Monkey Hypothesis explains why. I should point out, though, that not every biologist agrees. And there are even those who think that evolution is bunk and that we were created instead by a benevolent deity. Creationists and evolutionists have an uncivilized tendency to squabble, but their different journeys come to the same destination. Benjamin Franklin, Founding Father of the United States, famously observed that the existence of wine was "proof that God loves us, and loves to see us happy." But in the same letter he made a significant observation about human anatomy:

To confirm still more your piety and gratitude to Divine Providence, reflect upon the situation which it has given to the *elbow*. You see in animals who are intended to drink the waters that flow upon the earth, that if they have long legs, they have also a long neck, so that they can get at their drink without kneeling down. But man, who was destined to drink wine, is framed in a manner that he may raise the glass to his mouth. If the elbow had been placed nearer the hand, the part in advance would have been too short to bring the glass up to the mouth; and if it had been nearer the shoulder, that part would have been so long, that when it attempted to carry the wine to the mouth it would have overshot the mark, and gone beyond the head . . . But from the actual situation of the elbow we are enabled to drink at our ease, the glass going directly to the mouth. Let us, then, with glass in hand, adore this benevolent wisdom;—let us adore and drink!

Franklin also argued that Noah's Flood was intended to punish mankind for drinking water, by trying to drown us in the stuff. But whichever way you slice it—evolution or the divine—we are designed to drink.

CHAPTER 2

THE PREHISTORY OF DRINKING

Anatomically modern humans (like you) have been around for 150,000 years and the first 125,000 of those were pretty much a disaster. So far as anyone can tell, there was no proper booze. It's all a bit uncertain, of course, as prehistoric humans didn't take notes. They were too busy hunting and gathering and painting their caves.

The first glimmer of hope was a lady called the Venus of Laussel. About 25,000 years ago somebody did a carving of a lady with huge breasts and a big belly who *appears* to be holding a drinking horn up to her mouth. Not everybody agrees that it's a drinking horn. Some people think that it's a musical instrument and that the poor girl was simply confused about which end to blow. Other archaeologists think that it has something to do with menstruation. Of course, even if it is a drinking horn, it might contain only water. But that seems unlikely as water-drinking isn't usually something you carve in stone for all eternity. We shall, alas, never know.

We shall also never know whether alcohol was being made at the time, or whether it was just being found. Most of the early drinks wouldn't so much have been invented as

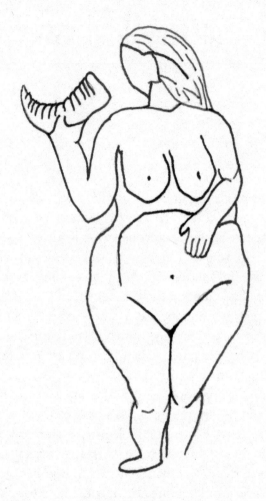

The Venus of Laussel, limestone relief,
France c. 25,000 years ago.

discovered. A pleasant theory involves bees. Imagine a bees' nest in the hollow of a tree. Then there's a storm, the tree falls over and the nest is flooded with rainwater. So long as you have roughly one part honey to two parts rainwater, fermentation ought to kick in pretty soon. So if, a few days later, a thirsty and primordially sober human happens to wander past they'll find something rather wonderful: natural mead. They'd probably try it too, as humans are very fond of honey. This will taste just like honey, but it'll get you drunk.

It's just a theory, but it's a nice one. More prosaically you simply need to be picking and storing fruit somewhere reasonably watertight. The juice at the bottom will start to bubble and pretty soon you'll have a very primitive wine. For that you would probably need pottery. More importantly you need to remain in the same place for a while, and all of the evidence suggests that our ancestors were mostly on the move.

So why did we settle down? The traditional line is that we did so in order to grow food. Then maybe we started to make drinks. And then we started to build great big temples and became civilized. This makes sense on the face of it, but could well be utterly wrong.

The oldest known building is a place called Göbekli Tepe in Turkey. It's a funny place because it didn't have a proper roof or walls, and there's no evidence at all that people ever lived there. Nor are there any traces of residential properties thereabouts. This makes sense as Göbekli Tepe dates from about 10,000 BC, which is before humans settled down to agriculture. So the place appears to have been made by hunter-gatherers as a kind of temple. It's a big place and the slabs of stone used to make it weighed up to 16 tons. So a lot of different tribes would have to have gathered there to put it all together.

Why would they do that?

There are some big stone tubs in Göbekli Tepe—the biggest held about 40 gallons—and they contain traces of a chemical called oxalate, which is formed when barley and water are mixed. When barley and water are mixed, beer quite naturally ferments. So it would appear that Göbekli Tepe was some sort of meeting place where the tribes gathered and drank beer together. It would be a pleasant place to get whiffled: top of a hill, nice view.

There are other theories of course. There usually are. Some say that the beer was to pay for the building work. Others say that there wasn't any beer at all, and maybe they just liked mixing water and barley in big vats because they liked their barley a bit soggy, and that they would surely have removed it before it could start to bubble and turn into delicious epipaleolithic ale.

But it looks like there was beer, and, importantly, it looks like there was beer before there were temples and before there was farming. This leads to the great theory of human history: that we didn't start farming because we wanted food—there was loads of that around. We started farming because we wanted booze.

This makes a lot more sense than you might think, for six reasons. First, beer is easier to make than bread as no hot oven is required. Second, beer contains vitamin B, which humans require if they're going to be healthy and strong. Hunters get their vitamin B by eating other animals. On a diet of bread and no beer, grain farmers will all turn into anemic weaklings and be killed by the big healthy hunters. But fermentation of wheat and barley produces vitamin B.

Third, beer is simply a better food than bread. It's more nutritious because the yeast has been doing some of the digesting for you. Fourth, beer can be stored and consumed later. Fifth, the alcohol in beer purifies the water that was used to make it, killing all the nasty microbes. The big problem with settling down is that you have to go to poo somewhere, and then little bits of that poo find their way into the water and then straight back into your mouth. This is not a problem faced by nomads.

The sixth and biggest argument, though, is that to really change behavior you need a cultural driver. If beer was worth traveling for (which Göbekli Tepe suggests it was) and if beer was a religious drink (which Göbekli Tepe suggests it was), then even the most ardent huntsman might be persuaded to settle down and grow some good barley to brew it with.

And so in about 9000 BC, we invented farming because we wanted to get drunk on a regular basis. This resulted in two things. First, we start to get proper, indubitable archaeological evidence of booze. Wine is good for this as it leaves a residue of tartaric acid. It's been found in China and dated to 7000 BC. It's been found a little later in Iran and then spreads westward to the Mediterranean. Of course, the progress may have gone the other way. These are just little archaeological whispers in the midst of a great silence.

The second, and much less important, result was civilization.

CHAPTER 3

SUMERIAN BARS

Cities are the result of farmers working too hard. In fact, history is the result of farmers working too hard. If you have a job that doesn't involve food-production (and you're alive), that means that somewhere there's a farmer producing more food than he needs. The second that happens you get specialized jobs, because ultimately you've got to be providing something to the farmer in exchange for the food, whether it's clothes or housing or protection or accountancy services. The sure sign of agricultural surplus is that there are populated places that produce no food at all. Such places are called cities, inhabited by citizens.

The Latin for citizen was *civis*, and from that we get the words *civil* and *civilization*.

When we give the farmers something in return, it's called trade, and trade causes disputes, and the people who solve these disputes are called the government. The government requires money to spend on important things like thrones, armies and fact-finding trips. And because it's terribly hard to remember who's paid their tax and who hasn't, tax requires writing. Writing causes Prehistory to stop, and History to begin.

All of this happened rather suddenly in the late fourth millennium BC in what's now Iraq, was once called Mesopotamia, and which was also called Sumeria, as Sumerian was the name of the language. Anyway, they invented civilization and it's been downhill ever since.

Pretty much the first thing people wrote about was beer. Very primitive writing was really just a bunch of IOUs. But there were no coins. People paid each other with barley, gold or beer. Originally, in about 3200 BC, you drew a little picture of a conical beer jug. That quickly got stylized into something that was easier to carve in clay; and in the same way that the men and women signs on lavatory doors no longer look like actual human beings, the symbol for beer was soon just a few lines scratched on a tablet. It could be used to mean beer, or it could be used just to refer to the sound of the word for beer, which was *kash*, and thus it became a letter.

This meant that the Mesopotamians were able to start writing more than IOUs; they could write about everything that they thought was important, which was, in general, god and beer. They also wrote about Ninkasi, who was the goddess of beer. She spent her time perpetually and eternally brewing. There's a hymn to her that explains how she moves the beer-dough about with a big shovel and dries it in an oven, and soaks it in a jar and adds sweetwort and honey and wine and so on and so forth. It's uncertain *exactly* how the Sumerians made their beer, but it certainly involved a lot of specialized pots, as we shall see later.

Everybody drank beer. Kings drank it on their thrones.

Priests drank it in temples. The first known poet of all history was a lady called Enheduanna. She was the daughter of Sargon the Great and he had her installed as the high priestess of a temple in the city of Ur. She decided to follow the rule of write-what-you-know-about and produced a collection of poems praising temples in and around Ur. They said things like:

> at your gate facing toward Iri-kug, wine is poured into holy An's beautiful bowls set out in the open air. Whatever enters you is unequaled, whatever leaves endures . . . terrifying façade, house of radiance, a place of reaching judgment which Lord Ninĝirsu has filled with great awesomeness and dread! All the Anuna gods attend your great drinking-bouts.

Or:

> O Isin, city founded by An which he has built on an empty plain! Its front is mighty, its interior is artfully built, its divine powers are divine powers which An has determined. Shrine which Enlil loves, place where An and Enlil determine destinies, place where the great gods dine, filled with great awesomeness and terror: all the Anuna gods attend your great drinking-bouts.

To be honest, her poetry could get a bit samey. I doubt she'd even have been published if her father hadn't been emperor of the known world. *Plus ça change.*

The point is that beer was considered important and

holy and sacred. There was a myth that civilization had only come about through beer. The story went that Enki, the god of wisdom, had sat down with the goddess of hanky-panky, whose name was Inana. At the time, humans had no skills or knowledge.

> So it came about that Enki and Inana were drinking beer together in the *abzu*,* and enjoying the taste of sweet wine. The bronze *aga* vessels were filled to the brim, and the two of them started a competition, drinking from the bronze vessels of Uraš.

Long story short: Inana wins. While Enki is passed out drunk, she steals all the wisdom from heaven and takes it down to earth. When Enki wakes up, he notices that all the wisdom is missing and throws a fit, but by then it's too late.

The most famous Sumerian myth of all, *The Epic of Gilgamesh*, starts with a wild man called Enkidu who lives among the animals like a Mesopotamian Mowgli, until a priestess of Inana turns up and tries to make him human. She does this by having sex with him, and then giving him a drink (not the usual order). Enkidu downs seven jugs of wine and loves it. Then he tries to return to his animal friends, but they don't want to be his friend anymore. So he goes to Uruk and wrestles with King Gilgamesh and becomes friends with him instead. Then he dies. There's a moral in there somewhere, but I can't fathom it.

---

* The great, mythological underground ocean.

The important thing is that beer was everywhere. It was what made you human, it was what made you civilized. There was a Sumerian proverb, "He is fearful, like a man unacquainted with beer," but a more revealing one just says, "Not to know beer is not normal."

So how did the average Sumerian get jolly? Let us say that we're travelers and we've arrived in the city of Ur in southern Iraq in around 2000 BC.* We have no interest in the ziggurat or seeing the sights, we want to get drunk. What do we do? We are neither potentates nor priests, so the palace and temple aren't a good starting place. What we need is a tavern. Luckily for us, such things exist and we just need to find one.

Taverns were usually somewhere near the main square, but as this is the largest city in the world, with a staggering 65,000 inhabitants (over half the size of Provo!), there are probably loads of them. The way to recognize a tavern is that it's got prostitutes hanging around outside the door. How do we recognize a prostitute? Well, they're wearing just a single garment, and they may well have a string of pearls around their neck. This is not necessarily because prostitutes in Ur were rich, it's just that there were fewer people back then, and more oysters.

So we set off through the streets of low, mud-brick buildings with their flat roofs and bingo. In the door we go. The first thing we notice as we get inside is that it's dark, there is a pungent smell, and it's full of flies. This is

* It wasn't called Iraq back then, it was called . . . well, it was called Ur. Also, nobody knew that it was 2000 BC.

because the beer is being brewed on site. Wine, if there is any, will have been imported from the countryside. The beer is being made right here, and that smell is the malt and barley and all the other stuff used in brewing.

As our eyes grow accustomed to the dark, we'll see the apparatus: a series of troughs and pots and pans all with special names. There's the *gakkul* vat and the *lamsare* vat and the straw troughs and the *ugurbal* jar. (These were all used in the brewing process, but archaeologists are a bit hazy on what exactly did what.) If we're in a reasonably posh place these may even be nicely decorated earthenware. But we're probably not.

Who's here? There are a lot of references in Sumerian literature to prostitutes outside the tavern door, but only one to a prostitute inside and in that passage she's sneaked in through the window. So this is not some heaving fleshpot. There is at least one woman here, but she's the owner.

Taverns were always owned by women. This is implied in the Sumerian Kings List, which is a list of semilegendary kings of Mesopotamia. There is only one queen: Kuababa, the tavern keeper who ruled Kish for a hundred years (I did say it was semilegendary). A female tavern keeper makes sense as brewing beer was a domestic chore, it was woman's weary work. That the owners were women is confirmed much more precisely by the law code of Hammurabi. This won't actually be written for another 300 years, but let that slide. Hammurabi makes three references to taverns:

108. If a tavern keeper [feminine noun] does not accept corn according to gross weight in payment of drink, but

takes money, and the price of the drink is less than that of the corn, she shall be convicted and thrown in the water [i.e., drowned].

109. If conspirators meet in the house of a tavern keeper [feminine], and these conspirators are not captured and delivered to the court, the tavern keeper shall be put to death.

110. If a "sister of a god" open a tavern, or enter a tavern to drink, then shall this woman be burned to death.

Let's deal with those three slightly out of order. First, the conspirators. Taverns were rather dodgy places. They were dark little bars just off the street where people could meet and plot and do illicit deals and complain about the government. If we look around our little drinking den, we'll probably see some people who fit the description.

Second, the "sister of a god," which just means a priestess. Taverns were not places for nice girls. This doesn't mean that there were no women in there at all. It's just not necessarily where you want your daughter to spend her time. There's another Sumerian proverb that goes:

The palace cannot avoid the wasteland. A barge cannot avoid straw. A freeborn man cannot avoid forced labor. A king's daughter cannot avoid the tavern.

It's not quite clear what this proverb *means*, but it appears to be something along the lines of "things always end up in the wrong place." And if the king's daughter is in here we should give her a wide, wide berth. No use getting in trouble.

So much for the clientele. They're a mixed bunch. Let us order some beer. The important thing is that we need to remember part 108 of Hammurabi's law code. The tavern mistress may well try to give us a short measure. If she does, we'll report her and she'll be drowned.

The Sumerians had quite a few different kinds of beer: there was barley beer, emmer-wheat beer, brown beer, dark beer, light beer, red beer, sweet beer, beer with honey and all sorts of other spices, strong beer mixed with wine and filtered beer. These last two would be very expensive, and it's perfectly possible that there would be one variety: the one they were making today. But it's also just possible that ancient Ur would be the perfect place for the craft-ale snob. Every pub was what we would now call a microbrewery. In fact, there were no macrobreweries at all. This means that, if you are so minded, you may now engage the tavern keeper in an earnest and endless conversation about how malty the brew is and complicated stuff about maceration and whatnot. You could even demand that your emmer-wheat beer "fizz like the water of the Papsir canal."*

We've then got to pay. The locals will be running a tab that's measured in barley. This is a barter society. Big purchases, like a house, could be paid by weighing out silver, but beer is cheap. You'd need a microscope to measure out the price of a beer in silver. So, as travelers, we have to

* I've no idea why a canal would fizz.

have something that we can exchange, presumably in a haggle. Probably some sort of spice we've picked up along the way. It could be anything. It could be a piglet. But we'll come back to that.

So now we sit down at a table and the beer is brought to us in an *amam* jar, along with two straws. Beer has to be drunk through a straw. This is because Sumerian beer is not like our lovely modern clear amber nectar. It's a sort of fizzing barley porridge with lots of solid stuff floating on the surface. A straw lets us go below the surface and suck out the sweet liquid. There are lots of representations of Sumerians doing this, and people still do it with palm wine in parts of central Africa.

We've got the beer. We've got the straws. What do we do now? Well, drinking competitions seem to have been standard practice. There are several mentions of the gods having drinking competitions, so we've got to assume that they existed among humans. People drank to get drunk. There are proverbs that mention this: "You should not pass judgment when you drink beer" and "You should not boast like a deceitful man: then your words will be trusted." If you have to condemn something, it's because people are doing it. The sins of a society are revealed in its pieties. So, as we compete to see who can drink the most, we shall boast, and deceive, and pass judgment.

Beer drinking was a happy communal thing. We'll probably make friends with the conspirators at the next table. We'll probably tell jokes. The Sumerians liked jokes. They made lists of them and some are still recognizably

Sumerians drinking beer through straws to avoid the sediment. Detail from the cylinder seal of Queen Puabi of Ur, c. 2600 BC.

funny, or sort of funny, today. "The dog gnawing on a bone says to his anus: 'This is going to hurt you!'" Or "Something which has never occurred since time immemorial: a young woman did not fart in her husband's embrace."

Sort of funny.

Sometimes lines have survived that are clearly jokes, but which we can no longer get. For example, "A dog walked into a tavern and said, 'I can't see a thing. I'll open this one.'" Why that's funny has been lost in a mist of 4,000 years. It is, nonetheless, the very earliest example of the *animal-walks-into-a-bar* joke. Some things never change.

We drink. We get drunk. We tell jokes. And it's probably at about this time that we should return to the subject of the prostitutes at the tavern door. This is not because prostitution is good or anything like that. But it was clearly a part of Sumerian drinking culture. We know very little about the process of the price. There's a hymn to Inana, the aforementioned goddess of nooky, in which she explains her pricing system:

When I stand up against the wall, it is 1 shekel; when I bend over, it is 1½ shekels.

That may not tell us much about pricing. Inana was, after all, a goddess, and could therefore charge extra. It does suggest, though, that you're not going to get a nice featherbed. The sex is strictly alfresco. The only realistic pricing guide to a human comes from a legal document that records one bout of sex in exchange for one piglet. A piglet was probably way too much to exchange for a single beer, so you could probably tell a customer's intentions early in the evening. If he was carrying a piglet, he wasn't just here for the booze.

But it's getting late. Everyone is pickled and it is time to finish up the evening with a drinking song. Beer was happy and beer was communal and beer led to sing-alongs. The words of one drinking song survive. It has rather a lot in it about all those mysterious pots and pans used for brewing, and a couple of mentions of the goddesses of beer and sex—Ninkasi and Inana. I've tinkered with the words a little, but not very much, just to make the lyrics rhyme. The following is a real Sumerian song. So if you imagine the lot of us, the travelers, the conspirators, the tavern mistress, the pearl-bedecked whore and the piglet, all arm in arm and singing away, it went like this:*

> The *gakkul* vat!
> The *gakkul* vat!
> The *gakkul* vat!
> The *lamsare* vat!
> The *gakkul* vat,
> Which makes sure that
> We're happy!

* Though it's musicologically anachronistic, I find that this fits roughly with the nursery rhyme "This Old Man Came Rolling Home."

33

The *lamsare* vat,
We're pleased with that.
But the *ugurbal* jar,
Is the best by far!

The *saggub* jar is filled with beer.
The *amam* jar brings it over here.
The troughs and the pails and the pots and the pans
Are all laid out on their neat pot-stands.

May the heart of your god be on your side,
The *gakkul* vat is our heart and guide.
It's good for you and it's good for me
And it makes us sing so merrily!

If you've spilled your beer on the tavern floor
You'll be happy with Ninkasi for evermore.
We'll live in peace and we'll do just fine
For we love the sound of her beer and wine.

All of the troughs are filled with beer
And the boys and the brewers and the bearers are here.
I'm spinning around on a beery lake
I'm feeling great, I'm feeling great.

I'm drinking beer in a blissful mood
I feel so fine drinking what's been brewed.
I'm happy in my body both up and down
And my heart is robed in a regal gown.

The heart of Inana is happy again.
The heart of Inana is happy again.

O, Ninkasi!

And then it's time to totter home through the silent streets, and console ourselves with the thought that, whatever we got up to, and whether or not it involved the expense of a piglet, we are at least a lot better behaved than the Ancient Egyptians.

CHAPTER 4

ANCIENT EGYPT

If you come home drunk and lie on the bed,
I'll rub your feet.

Egyptian love poem (late New Kingdom)

The Ancient Egyptians were a funny lot. They spent less money on their palaces than on their graves; they thought that the world had been created by a god committing a solitary sexual act and accidentally getting some in his own mouth; and they thought that beer had saved humanity.

The myth went something like this. Mankind had been saying nasty things about Ra, who was the top god (and the one mentioned in the previous paragraph). For some reason mankind was often doing this in Egyptian myth and it never ended well. Ra blew his top and decided that it was time to kill the whole lot of them. So he sent the goddess Hathor to do it. Hathor had the head of a lion and the temper of a shih tzu, and she went at it with gusto.

She slaughtered here and she slaughtered there until Ra started to feel sorry for mankind and decided to let them live. But Hathor was having none of it. Her blood was up and she was of the opinion that, if a job was worth doing, it was worth finishing.

Ra found himself in a bit of a pickle. So he quickly made 7,000 kegs of beer and dyed it red. Then he poured it over the fields. Hathor saw the beer, assumed that it was human blood and began to drink it. Soon she became sleepy, forgot about her divine killing spree and settled down for a nap. And thus mankind was saved by beer.

For some reason Ra then built a cow.

All of this led to the Festival of Drunkenness, which we shall come to in a minute. But before we go any further it's worthwhile pointing out a few oddities of Egyptian history. First, it went on for a very, very, very long time. Egypt was united in 3000 BC (or shortly before) and very quickly developed those two cornerstones of civilization: hieroglyphics and pyramids. It thus became the richest and most powerful nation on earth. With a couple of blips Egypt then held that position for the next 2,000 years. As of about 1000 BC the country went into a bit of a decline that lasted for the next thousand years and a bit. This all adds up to rather a long time.

Cleopatra may seem terribly ancient to us, but she died only 2,000 years ago. The Great Pyramid at Giza was built 2,500 years before she was born. That pyramid was more ancient to Cleopatra than she is ancient to us.

All this means that making generalizations about how the Ancient Egyptians got wasted is a trifle difficult. The first thousand years or so has very little evidence. We know that they were drinking. The workers who built the Great Pyramid were partly paid in beer. King Scorpion I who died around 3150 BC was buried with 300 jugs of imported wine, so we know they had that. Or at least the rich did.

The problem is that we don't know *how* Scorpion drank his wine. On his own? With friends? In one big binge? Or did he like to sip it? The pyramid workers, I expect, were just plain damned thirsty, as most of us would be if we were manual laborers in the Sahara.

So most of what follows is from the period we have good evidence for, which is the late New Kingdom, around 1200 BC.

Second, most of what we know about Ancient Egypt comes from the tombs of rich people. Some of it comes from poems and the like, which were written by rich people for rich people, and some of it comes from inscriptions in temples, which only rich people were allowed into. We know next to nothing about the Nilotic proletariat, except that they died young and didn't wear many clothes. Which leads to the third point.

When little schoolchildren learn about the Ancient Egyptians, their teachers never tell them about the sex. This is a jolly good thing. The myths of the Greeks and of the Romans can, with a little tweaking, make for a nice bedtime story; what Isis did to the dead body of her brother can't. As for the sacred text *The Contendings of Horus and Seth*, it would make the most jaded pornographer weep and long for his lost innocence. What follows is therefore pretty tame by Egyptian standards; indeed by Egyptian standards it's rather sweet.

Drink meant sex to Egyptians, and for that matter sex meant drink. And the two went perfectly with music. They wrote love poems that said things like:

> Give her dance and give her song,
> Give her wine and ale that's strong,
> Confuse her cunning and have her tonight
> And she will say "Dear, hold me tight.
> Let's do it again at morning light."

Or sometimes it's the woman who's getting the man drunk, because Egyptian women liked to drink a lot. They had a terribly modern gender equality in the business of getting tanked. There's a painting of a New Year's feast where the women are seated at a separate table from the men, but they're drinking just as much wine. Moreover, there's a caption giving us their dialogue. The butler is saying: "For your soul, drink until you are drunk. Make festival! Listen to what your relative tells you. Don't just sit there."

"Give me eighteen jars of wine," demands one old woman. "I always want to be drunk. My insides feel like straw."

The butler says to the next woman, "Drink! Don't sip. I shall stay beside you." (This isn't a euphemism. For once.)

And then a third woman pipes up and says, "Drink! Don't be annoying. Then pass me the cup."

The amount they want to drink is startling. But there are two extra points to notice. They are drinking with the sole and explicit aim of drunkenness. There is nothing calm or social about this. They want to get legless. That's why the butler says that he'll stay beside them. At an Egyptian drinking session, even one for respectable ladies, you had to have someone to make sure that you didn't topple into the Nile or drown in your own vomit.

And they did vomit rather a lot. In another banquet painting a woman is shown happily throwing up toward a waitress who's patting her on the head and still holding the wine cup toward her. This is proper, full-on binge drinking. It's quite hard to say whether Egyptians drank every day, or just at festivals (*happy days*, as they called them); but either way there were an awful lot of festivals.

These scenes are painted up in tombs, because Egyptians were proud of their binge drinking. There was no shame in getting sloshed. They wanted the memory of your sloshedness to live for all eternity. People were quite particular about it. Even a priest would write:

> Never did I forget the happy day when I commemorated those who rest in their tombs. Even more did I sit relaxing and I did "travel the marshes" in what I did being drunk with wine and beer, anointed with myrrh.

"Traveling the marshes" was the standard Ancient Egyptian term for having sex, because having sex was what you did when you were drunk, whether male or female. There was a lady called Chratiankh and all that we know about her is her boastful tomb inscription:

Detail from the tomb of Neferhotep c. 1300 BC.
The lady on the left is a servant holding a
wine vessel. The lady on the right is drunk.

I was a mistress of drunkenness, one who loved a good day, who looked forward to roaming the marshes every day, anointed with myrrh and perfumed with lotus scent.

She then goes on to say that she would travel the marshes with her husband while the beautiful maidservants played music. She next seems to imply that she had her wicked way with the maidservants too. That's Ancient Egypt for you.

All of which brings us to the Festival of Drunkenness. And now that you've had a little background, the following should be rather less surprising.

The Festival of Drunkenness was a yearly (or possibly twice-yearly) celebration of the goddess Hathor* and the salvation of humankind through the miracle of beer. It coincided with the annual flooding of the Nile which brought fertility to Egypt and, according to legend, the return of Hathor from her exile in the far south. It took place at the temple of Hathor and was attended by crowds of rich Egyptians, including aristocrats and members of the royal family. It would have been quite a scene.

The festival began at dusk. The worshippers would be in a crowd on the eastern bank of the Nile as the sun set on the far side of the river. They were wearing their best clothes.

---

* Egyptian deities were weirdly fluid in their identities. They could become one another. So you could have Mut–Hathor or Hathor–Ai or Mut in her Hathor aspect, or Sekhmet, or Bastet. They could also change animal heads so Hathor could have the head of a lion if she was angry, or a cow, or a human. For simplicity, I'm just using the name Hathor.

The women would have on their *wah*-collars, like enormous necklaces. They had makeup around their eyes and garlands on their heads. Everybody was anointed, rubbed with sweet-smelling oil, and flowers were scattered everywhere to make the whole atmosphere smell like heaven.

Everyone was expectant. Behind them was the temple, waiting for her goddess to arrive. The temple was, as one poem puts it, "like a drunken woman / Seated outside the dwelling place [of god], / Her braided locks falling upon her beautiful breasts. / She has linen and sheets."

They were waiting for the ceremonial barge that would appear on the Nile sailing downstream toward them. Hathor was returning. Women would start to beat their hand-drums as the barge approached and docked. A priest would board the boat carrying with him a drinking bowl filled with red-dyed beer and present it to the goddess.

I'm afraid it's utterly unclear what this means. There may have been somebody dressed up as Hathor or there may have been a statue or it could have been something else. The important point is that Hathor drank (or a statue had some beer spilled on it), and at that moment a great cheer went up from the crowd.

The drummers drummed and Hathor disembarked. She was surrounded by a procession of priests and dancers, who did the traditional drinking dance: right arm raised and bent 90 degrees at the elbow. She had returned from the south and it *seems* that the dancers were dressed in animal costumes—baboons and monkeys to show that she was the mistress of all nature. Some may even have been dressed in the exotic clothes of Nubians.

The crowd parted and Hathor processed through the front gate into the temple's forecourt. Well, I say the crowd parted but they were still crowding. Everybody was trying to get a look and they would climb over the giant statues that flanked the entrance and sit on the gate's top to get a better view of what was going on. It was not a solemn occasion. It was disorderly. It was, after all, the Festival of Drunkenness.

In the temple forecourt you had the next stage of the ceremony: the striking of the balls. For once in Ancient Egypt, this wasn't sexual. The balls were made of earthenware and represented the eyes of the enemies of the goddess. As such they were bad things and a senior worshipper (the Pharaoh, if he was there) would hit them with a big stick. It's unclear exactly how he hit them. Whether he smashed them or tapped them symbolically. But as the balls were only about an inch across and the stick was a few feet long, I rather like to imagine it as an early version of golf.

Once the balls had been struck, the Pharaoh would go home, and the real fun would start. Huge amounts of wine and beer were handed around, but very little food. As before, this was drinking with only one aim in mind: sacred drunkenness, and to be a holy drunk you have to be wholly drunk.

Braziers illuminated the courtyard and the pillared hall as the wine bowls were handed around. People glugged it down with religious fervor. They got smashed. A priest stood on a podium and read out hymns. In case anybody wasn't sure why they were here, he would helpfully remind them:

Yes, let us drink and let us eat from the banquet!
Let us rejoice, rejoice, and rejoice again!
May Bastet* come to our feet!
Let us become drunk for her at her feast of drunkenness.

But he would also remind them of the other thing that they were expected to do:

Let him drink, let him eat, let him shag.

That last phrase is usually translated as "have sexual relations," but frankly in describing what happened next there's no room for prudery. Everybody shagged. It seems astonishing to our modern sensibilities, but the Egyptians were not modern or sensible. They were from a culture that loved and worshipped hanky-panky. They were all anointed with perfumed oil (over the whole body), the stars were out, the moon was (probably) up, and they were all utterly lashed. Moreover the priest was telling them to. So, yes, they shagged, right there in the temple hall. In fact, the hall was actually called the Hall of Traveling the Marshes.

This may sound strange, and you may be thinking to yourself, "What if somebody got pregnant?" They did. There was nothing wrong with being conceived in the drunken chaos of the festival, possibly fathered by a complete stranger. Such children were rather admired and when they grew up they not only had an entry into the priesthood, but they would brag about their origins. A chap with the easily

* By which he basically means Hathor. See previous footnote.

pronounceable name of Kenherkhepeshef put up a monument to himself (the Egyptians did stuff like that) which read:

> I was conceived in the forecourt, the portal beside Deir el-Bahari down toward Meniset. I ate the offering bread of the lector priests beside the great *Akhu*-spirits. I strolled in the Valley of the Queens. I spent the night in the forecourt. I drank the water, and the sight of the glowing one was transmitted in the forecourt of Menet.

Kenherkhepeshef was also the most favored child in his mother's will, so she clearly didn't mind. She may even have had fond memories of the event.

The much more practical problem of the orgy is how the sex worked with the vomiting. There was certainly quite a lot of this going on as it seems to have been considered, for some reason, a religious necessity.* Just in case you had a stomach that could take all that booze without it returning by the same route, they would add emetic herbs to the beer just to make sure. It's a shame because at the beginning of the evening everything would have smelled so lovely.

Finally, the worshippers did what everybody does after getting hideously drunk, vomiting and having sex with strangers: they fell asleep. By the last hours of the night the Hall of Drunkenness was filled with snoring and unconsciousness, and this is when the magic happened.

---

* Curiously, there's an Australian euphemism for drunken vomiting (into a lavatory bowl): "talking to God on the great white telephone." I'd like to think that this is significant here, but it probably isn't.

Some people had not got drunk. They had been waiting around, like the butler mentioned earlier, to help people who were helpless. Now, in the silence, they set about their final task. In a chapel at the side of the temple was a great grand statue of Hathor. They opened the doors and some-how (history does not relate) maneuvered the statue into the Hall of Drunkenness. They placed it right in the center of the room, and, as the first light of dawn pierced the pillared colonnade, they started drumming. It was a din of drums, tambourines and sistrums, and the aim was to wake everybody up *while they were still drunk.*

Anybody to whom something similar has happened will know the feeling of disorientation and confusion at being wakened rudely from a wine-drenched slumber. You don't know where you are, you're unsure who you are or precisely what you are. And in this case, there was the goddess towering above you, lit by the eastern sun.

This was the moment that the whole festival had been aiming toward, this was the mystical epiphany because in your befuddled state you experienced the goddess in a way that you couldn't on a sober weekday afternoon.

> When they are drunk, they will see the goddess
> By means of the vessel. Drink, truly. Eat, truly. Drink,
>   eat, sing,
> Get drunk.

And at this moment of perfect communion, anything that you ask of the goddess will be granted to you—although

I should imagine that quite a lot of people forgot what they wanted to ask her.

This all seems rather bizarre to us. There is, in the Western world, no tradition of religious drunkenness. But it is a practice found across history and across the globe. From Mexico to the Pacific islands to Ancient China there is or has been drunken mysticism, god found at the bottom of a bottle. For my own part, if I had a few snifters and suddenly beheld the spirits of my ancestors, I would be surprised to say the least (my ancestors, I'm afraid, would be gloomily resigned). So this is, perhaps, the hardest part of drunkenness for the thoroughly modern mixologist to grasp.

It's therefore probably worthwhile to quote here, in full, the words of William James, the great psychologist, philosopher and brother of Henry. In his analysis of religious mysticism he analyzes rather neatly the great part played by drunkenness that we secular fools have forgotten, but may with help remember:

The sway of alcohol over mankind is unquestionably due to its power to stimulate the mystical faculties of human nature, usually crushed to earth by the cold facts and dry criticisms of the sober hour. Sobriety diminishes, discriminates, and says no; drunkenness expands, unites, and says yes. It is in fact the great exciter of the *Yes* function in man. It brings its votary from the chill periphery of things to the radiant core. It makes him for the moment one with truth. Not through mere perversity do men run after it. To the poor and the unlettered it stands in the place of symphony concerts and of literature; and it is part of the deeper mystery and tragedy of life that whiffs and gleams of something that we immediately recognize as excellent should be vouchsafed to so many of us only in the fleeting earlier phases of what in its totality is so degrading a poisoning. The drunken consciousness is one bit of the mystic consciousness, and our total opinion of it must find its place in our opinion of that larger whole.

Or as the Egyptians put it:

For your soul! Drink, become perfectly drunk.

CHAPTER 5

THE GREEK SYMPOSIUM

There is, I take it, often sense in wine,
And those are stupid who on water dine.

Amphis of Athens (*c.* fourth century BC)

The Greeks didn't drink beer, they drank wine; but they watered it down by a ratio of about two or three parts water to one part wine, which made it almost exactly the same strength. That's the funny thing about the Greeks: they had to *complicate* everything. Still, this allowed them to indulge in their very favorite pastime, because more than anything else, more than philosophy or pederasty or drinking or sculpture, the Greeks loved being sniffy about foreigners.

The Persians drank beer; that made them barbarians. The Thracians drank undiluted wine; that made them barbarians. The Greeks were the only people who had it just right, according to the Greeks.

Given the Greek penchant for cocking a snook at those

who dared to be not-Greek, it's a little surprising that their god of wine, Dionysus, was usually said to be a foreigner. He was born on Mount Nysa, which was in either Ethiopia or Arabia, or sometimes India, and he had traveled to Greece from the East with a horde of exotic animals and dancing humans and centaurs and other mythical creatures.

(In fact, it's rather intriguing that the Greek god of wine and the Egyptian goddess of beer were both said to arrive from the exotic south with a dancing menagerie of humans, animals and spirits, but it's probably just a coincidence.)

Dionysus was, though, a Greek god. He's mentioned as far back as 1200 BC, and he pops up in the *Iliad*, so he'd been around for 700 years by the time you get to the fifth century BC, which is when Athens became classical, and when most of the stuff we think of as Ancient Greek actually happened.

The myths about Dionysus mostly fall into two categories.

(1) There are the stories of people who don't recognize him, and don't even realize that he is a god. Who these people are varies from pirates to princes, but their fate is usually the same. Dionysus punishes them by turning them into animals. The moral of the stories is reasonably clear. When you're dealing with wine you need to remember that you are dealing with something powerful, something divine. This is no ordinary drink. It is holy. Moreover, alcohol, if you're not careful, can bring out the beast in you.

Dionysus was always connected with animals. He had

a chariot pulled by lions and tigers. He hung around with centaurs, who are half human and half horse, and satyrs, who are half human and half goat. He had a human friend called Silenus, who nonetheless was sometimes depicted as having horse's ears and a tail. In fact, the only fully human friends he had were the maenads.

Maenads were women who worshipped Dionysus. They did this by going out into the mountains wearing next to nothing and getting very, very drunk. Then they would dance and let their hair down and rip animals to pieces in a sort of terrifying Arcadian hen party.

Nobody is quite sure whether maenads ever actually existed, or whether they were just a sexual fantasy of Greek men, like the Amazons. Greek women had a fine time mythologically, but in reality they tended to have to stay at home and were distinctly put upon. Of course, there may have been the occasional priestess here or there. There is one epitaph from the second century BC that goes:

Bacchae [maenads] of the city, say "Farewell, holy priestess." An excellent woman deserves this. She led you to the mountain and carried all the sacred objects and implements, processing at the head of the whole city.

But that's only one, and it may well have been just a disappointing ritual. Maenads seem unlikely: on a purely practical level, how would you transport all that booze up a mountain?

The maenads, though, were terribly important in the second type of Dionysus myth.

(2) Dionysus didn't like teetotalers. This is unsurprising for a god of wine, but Dionysus being Dionysus he tends to kill them cruelly. The most famous example is a play by Euripides where the King tries to outlaw maenadism so Dionysus makes his maenads believe that the King is a lion and they rip him limb from limb (the group is led by the King's mother). There's another story about Orpheus wandering the countryside. His wife has died and he wants to have a good cry. Unfortunately, he comes across a group of maenads who are all getting plastered and want him to join in. Orpheus politely declines and they rip him limb from limb as well.

There are a lot of stories like this and they all end the same way. The moral is pretty clear: you should recognize that drinking is dangerous and that it might turn you into a wild beast, but you should still drink. Never turn down an invitation to a party. Do not, whatever you do, try to ban drunkenness.

So, Greek mythology has a funny, rather wary relationship with drunkenness. The Sumerians saw it as a pure and jolly communal good, the Egyptians saw it as an extreme sport, but the Greeks stood back and stroked their beards and pondered. They developed theories and employed strategies. The Spartans, who were a nasty bunch, would force their slaves to get drunk in front of the children, in order to put them off the idea. The Athenians, who were a trifle less sadistic, decided to philosophize over exactly how drunk you should get and how you should behave when drunk.

Plato, quite specifically, says that getting drunk is like

going to the gym: the first time you do it you'll be really bad and end up in pain. But practice makes perfect. If you can drink a lot and still behave yourself, then you are an ideal man. If you can do this in company, then you can show the world that you are an ideal man, because you are displaying the great virtue of self-control even under the influence.

Self-control, said Plato, was like bravery. A man can only display bravery when he's in danger. A man can only display self-control when he's drunk a lot of wine. Bravery can be learned. A chap who spends his days fighting battles can train himself to be brave. A man who spends his evenings getting drunk can train himself to ever higher levels of self-control.

> What is better adapted than the festive use of wine, in the first place to test, and in the second place to train, the character of a man, if care be taken in the use of it? What is there cheaper, or more innocent?

Basically, Plato thought that if you can trust a fellow when he's drunk, you can trust him anywhere. Moreover, the drinking test has no real downside. If you get into a business deal with a man and then find out that he's dishonest, you lose money. But if you get drunk with him first you get to see his true character, without putting anything at risk.

All of which leads to the logical conclusion that you can't trust a teetotaler.

So drunkenness in Greece was a strange and subtle

business. You were meant to drink. You were meant to get drunk. But you were meant to know what you were doing. You were meant to display virtue in drunkenness, and sail a steady ship on a stormy sea of wine. And the venue for this was the symposium.

Symposium

Let us say that you were a lady in classical Athens and you wanted to get drunk. You couldn't. Women weren't allowed at symposiums. Or, to be more precise, women might be allowed but not ladies. The symposium took place in a private room in the house called the *andron*, which literally means the "men's room." The only girls you'd find in there were slaves: maybe a flute-player, maybe a dancer, maybe a prostitute. Sometimes she might have been a combination of all three. But she was not doing much boozing; she was, however you look at it, the entertainment.

So it was the men who gathered, and they gathered at somebody's private house. Not at a bar. For a typical symposium you might have a dozen chaps over. A really large one might be up to thirty fellows, but that was unusual. First, you had supper. This was a plain meal that was consumed pretty quickly and pretty silently. The food was not the thing—it was only really there to soak up the wine. The Athenians had their priorities right.

When supper was finished you went through to the *andron*. It was a round room at the center of the house with a stone floor that sloped slightly toward the center to let the slaves clean it more easily when the drinking was over. The walls were decorated with murals, usually with a drinking theme of some sort. Perhaps a maenad or two, or an evil teetotaler being ripped limb from limb.

Arranged in a circle around the room were couches with cushions on them. A couch usually held two men, so there were probably between six and twelve of them. The men would lie down on the couches with a pillow under one arm. Young men, though, were not allowed to lie down. They had to drink sitting up straight. Exactly when a fellow was deemed old enough to lie down like a grown-up varied. In Macedonia you could lie down once you had killed your first wild boar.

It may then have been necessary to choose a symposiarch—the leader of the evening's drinking. This would almost always be the host, but if for some strange reason it wasn't, he would be chosen by drawing lots or rolling dice. The symposiarch's first job was to choose the wine. Usually, this would be from his private estate as most Athenian gentlemen would own a vineyard, indeed the class system in Athens was built around how big your vineyard was. The lowest level was 7 acres or less; the highest had over 25.

If it was summer, the wine would have been cooled by lowering it into a well, or burying it, or, if you were very, very posh, covering it in imported snow and straw. If you were very, very posh, the wine itself might have been imported. The very finest wine was from Lesbos.

So the wine was brought in in a big vat called a krater,

which was carried by two slaves. They then fetched the hydria, which was full of water, and poured it into the krater at a ratio of about three parts water to one part wine. The resulting mixture was then put into jugs which were used to fill the shallow, two-handled drinking bowls that people could finally take a swig from.

Except you couldn't. First of all, they had to have a libation. A libation is when perfectly good wine is poured onto the floor in honor of the gods. In Athens, they began a symposium with three libations. The first was to all the gods, the second was to fallen heroes, especially if they were your ancestors, and the third was to Zeus, the king of the gods. Each one was accompanied by a prayer recited by the symposiarch. Flowers and perfume might also have been handed around, and by the time it's all finished you were probably itching for a drink.

The biggest difference between the way the Athenians drank and the way we do is that they were deliberate. At a modern party in the Western world you may get drunk by mistake, you may have one too many. Nobody ever got drunk at a symposium by accident. At a symposium you got deliberately, methodically and publicly drunk. Everybody was given a bowl of wine. Everybody had to drink their bowl of wine before there's a refill. Failure to do so was unmanly and rude. When the symposiarch said drink, you drank.

That doesn't mean that the symposiarch wanted everybody to binge. He was in charge and it was his decision whether this evening was going to be a slow, mild session or a debauched binge. The important thing is that it's up to him, and not up to the guests.

This, incidentally, is why the most famous symposium in history was not a proper symposium. Plato's *Symposium* starts off with the host complaining that he's still hung over from the night before:

> libations were offered, and after a hymn had been sung to the god, and there had been the usual ceremonies, they were about to commence drinking, when Pausanias said, And now, my friends, how can we drink with least injury to ourselves? I can assure you that I feel severely the effect of yesterday's potations, and must have time to recover.

And this leads to an extraordinary decision:

> It was agreed that drinking was not to be the order of the day, but that they were all to drink only so much as they pleased.

This would have been pretty shocking to an Athenian, which is why Plato has to spell it out. Drinking was to be "voluntary." Most uncivilized. They even decide to do without the female flute-player.

Now the conversation could begin, but not in the way that we might expect it. Just as the guests at a symposium didn't get to choose how much they drank, so they didn't get to choose what they talked about, or indeed if they talked at all. The symposiarch would name a subject and then each guest in turn would have to give their opinion on it. In Plato's *Symposium* the subject is love. Xenophon wrote a similar story in which the subject is "what are you most proud of?," but in both each guest is meant to launch into a long and detailed answer.

There were almost certainly lowbrow symposiums in which the subject was "tell a dirty joke," but it seems that the form would have been the same. There would be none of the free flow of conversation that we associate with a drinking session, and no opportunity simply to remain silent. One guest tries this in Xenophon's story, and Socrates gets quite angry with him. Of course, the formality may have waned as the evening went on, but it would still have struck us as weirdly formal, like a game with strict rules.

In fact, there was an actual game that Athenians played at symposiums. It was called *kottabos*. You took the last few drops of wine in your drinking bowl and tried to flick it at something. Sometimes a special bronze target would be brought in and everyone would flick their wine at it. Sometimes the target was a bowl floating in a pot of water and your aim was to sink it. Sometimes the target was a person. It all sounds rather messy, and old people used to complain about it and say that young men should be doing something constructive instead.

But if the symposiarch wanted to play *kottabos*, you had to play *kottabos*. It's uncertain how long this dictatorial control would have lasted. Wine doesn't like a leader, and drunkenness tends to democracy. At some point the alcohol would have triumphed over the discipline. When one krater of wine was finished, he would order another to be brought in and, in the end, it would necessarily become chaotic. A playwright called Eubulus described it like this:

For sensible men I prepare only three kraters: one for health (which they drink first), the second for love and pleasure, and the third for sleep. After the third one is drained, wise men go home.

The fourth krater is not mine any more—it belongs to bad behavior; the fifth is for shouting; the sixth is for rudeness and insults; the seventh is for fights; the eighth is for breaking the furniture; the ninth is for depression; the tenth is for madness and unconsciousness.

Madness may seem a rather strong word, but the Greeks really did believe that alcohol, taken in very large quantities, made you mad. And, perhaps because they believed it, it seems to have happened. A historian called Timaeus of Tauromenium tells this story, which looks very odd to us, but was clearly convincing to the Greeks:

there was a certain house at Acragas called the Trireme [a kind of boat], on this account:—Some young men got drunk in it, and got so mad when excited by the wine, as to think that they were sailing in a trireme, and that they were being tossed about on the sea by a violent storm; and so completely did they lose their senses, that they threw all the furniture, and all the sofas and chairs and beds, out of the window, as if they were throwing them into the sea, fancying that the captain had ordered them to lighten the ship because of the storm. And though a crowd collected round the house and began to plunder what was thrown out, even that did not cure the young men of their frenzy. And the next day, when the generals came to the house, there were the young men still lying, seasick as they said; and, when the magistrates questioned them, they replied that they had been in great danger from a storm, and had consequently been compelled to lighten the ship by throwing all their superfluous cargo into the sea. And while the magistrates marveled at the bewilderment of the men, one of them, who seemed to be older than the rest, said, "I, O Tritons, was so frightened that I threw myself down under the benches, and lay there as low down and as much out of sight as I could." And the magistrates forgave their folly, and dismissed them with a reproof, and a warning not to indulge in too much wine in future. And they, professing to be much obliged to them, said, "If we arrive in port after having escaped this terrible storm, we will erect in our own country statues of you as our saviors in a conspicuous place, along with those of the other gods of the sea, as having appeared to us at a seasonable time." And from this circumstance that house was called the Trireme.

Not every symposium ended like this, but, if you believe that alcohol will send you mad, it will. If you believe that alcohol will make you hallucinate, it will.

A symposium could end in other ways. You could go home quietly or you could notice that the great thing about getting soused on a couch is that you can go to sleep then and there. Sometimes, it all ended in a *komos*, where you all ran through the street shouting and whooping and deliberately waking up the neighbors. Xenophon ends his symposium with everyone heading home in high spirits and carriages; Plato ends his with everybody lying around smashed except for Socrates, who's stone cold sober.

It's a strange thing that all the historians and philosophers seem to agree on: Socrates drank huge amounts and never got drunk. Perhaps he really did have a soul so well ordered that drunkenness revealed nothing but his rationality. Or perhaps he had a freakishly efficient liver. Either way, he seems to be the first of many men praised for the peculiar reason that he could drink without getting drunk.

This is, if you think about it, rather an odd thing to be proud of, or even pleased about. Imagine somebody boasting that LSD never made them hallucinate. You might well be puzzled and politely inquire why they bothered taking it if it didn't alter their consciousness.

But alcohol is different and throughout history we'll see people who are proud that drink has no effect on them, who are admired for it, who boast about it. We say what a *strong* head they have. We respect them, we admire them, we listen to their opinions. And nobody ever seems to say, "So why do you bother drinking?"

CHAPTER 6

ANCIENT CHINESE DRINKING

He who dreams of drinking wine may weep when morning comes.

Zhuangzi (*c.* fourth century BC)

Wine was first made in China by Yi Di in about 2070 BC. He presented his invention to the first Chinese Emperor, Yu. Yu drank it, liked it, but, being a Wise Emperor, realized that it would cause dreadful disasters and calamities. So he banned it, and exiled Yi Di for good measure.

Unfortunately that story isn't at all true. Early Chinese history is a bunch of very pretty myths with very little evidence. Writing wasn't properly invented in China until about 1200 BC. Before that you have to rely on archaeology. Oddly enough, the earliest known wine, indeed the earliest alcohol that we know about for absolute certain, was found in Jiahu in China and dated to about 7000 BC.

There was almost certainly no Emperor Yu and no Yi Di. But they're worth talking about because they are legends that illustrate the Ancient Chinese attitude to booze, which was, roughly, "This is rather nice, but also rather dangerous, and it should probably be illegal."

The last emperor of the dynasty founded by Yu was a funny chap called Jie (1728–1675 BC, allegedly). Jie was a Bad Emperor because he was much too fond of booze. He loved the stuff, but he had a peculiar habit. He insisted that when he was drinking he had to be riding on somebody else's back like a horse. We all, I suppose, have our eccentricities, but Jie's became problematic because he drank all the time, and it became tiring for the people beneath him. One day, for example, he was happily drinking and riding his chancellor around like a horse when his chancellor became exhausted and collapsed, so Jie had him executed.

Jie had a favorite courtesan called Mo Xi, who was also an alcoholic. She had the fantastic idea of constructing a whole lake of wine. One was duly dug and she and Jie paddled around it in a canoe while lots of naked girls and boys swam around having an orgy. But Mo Xi got bored and ordered 3,000 men to try to drink the whole lake dry. She then laughed uproariously when they all drowned.

Then there was a series of natural disasters and a chap called Tang of Shang rose up, defeated the Evil Emperor and established the Shang Dynasty. The Shang Dynasty is much less legendary than the Xia because it lasted all the way up to 1046 BC. But it's still not very reliably documented. The last Shang Emperor was Di Xin, who was a Bad Emperor because he was much too fond of booze.

He had a lake dug, filled with wine (he was under the influence of his evil wife), and he was fond of orgies etc., etc., until a good chap rose up and overthrew him. The only significant difference between Di Xin and Jie is that Di Xin's lake had an island in the middle with artificial trees that were hung with cooked meat, so he could paddle around, drink wine and pick bacon. This is called Progress.

Di Xin probably did exist, but the lake probably didn't. The important thing is that the Chinese considered drunkenness to be something that could bring down whole dynasties, that could disturb the order of the kingdom; and the Chinese were very, very concerned with keeping their kingdoms orderly.

There may actually be a dreg of truth in the story of the wine lake. The number of ceremonial bronze drinking vessels that archaeologists have dug up drops off sharply at the end of the Shang Dynasty, which implies that the next lot were much more sober. These drinking vessels were used in ceremonies to worship and make contact with your dead ancestors. The details are a little hazy. It seems that wine and food were put on an altar, libations were poured onto the ground, and the participants would then drink themselves into some sort of ecstatic religious state where the ancestral spirits would communicate with them. The ancestral spirits would be drunk as well, indeed the ceremony concluded with the words "The spirits are all drunk," at which point the ritual was over and you could start to feast.

There's a document from the early first millennium

BC called the *Proclamation Concerning Drunkenness*. It's interesting because it says that Di Xin *was* a drunkard, and that the Shang Dynasty fell because everyone was drinking.

> When Heaven sends down its terrors, and our people are thereby greatly disorganized and lose their virtue, this may be traced invariably to their indulgence in wine; yea, the ruin of states, small and great (by these terrors), has been caused invariably by their guilt in the use of wine.

The *Proclamation* bans drinking anywhere other than at rituals and finishes off with:

> If you are informed that there are companies that drink together, do not fail to apprehend them all, and send them here to Kâu, where I may put them to death.

It doesn't seem to have worked. There are an awful lot of ancient Chinese edicts banning drinking, so many that you can be sure that they were ineffectual. As I've mentioned before, things are only banned when people are doing them. So a lot of bans implies a lot of booze. But, importantly, there remained an absolute opposition between social order and political stability on the one side and anarchic alcohol on the other.

The Chinese solution to this was, basically, Confucian. Confucius (551–479 BC) died just before the Warring States period of Chinese history, which was pretty much as the name suggests. There was chaos and bloodshed and everybody wanted to know how to make people calm down. Confucius reckoned that the way to do it was ritual and ceremony. The basic idea is that if you spend all day bowing to your superiors, you'll get so used to it that it will seem perfectly natural that they are your superiors. The same goes for any part of social life: if you have enough formal etiquette, rigorously enforced, people will fall into line. They'll internalize (to use the modern term) all of the ceremonials of the outside world, and the result will be peace and plenty. Confucius would never sit on his mat when it was wonky. He considered this important.

It's therefore rather surprising that Confucius drank as much as he liked, but, like Socrates, he *never got drunk*:

> [Confucius] did not eat meat which was not cut properly, nor what was served without its proper sauce. Though there might be a large quantity of meat, he would not allow what he took to exceed the due proportion for the rice. It was only in wine that he laid down no limit for himself, but he did not allow himself to be confused by it. He did not partake of wine and dried meat bought in the market. He was never without ginger when he ate. He did not eat much.

But for others there were limits. Nobody should drink until their parents had been fed. Order and self-control were paramount. And in the more general movement that Confucius represented, the control of alcohol was vital. A book called the *Yue Ji* from roughly the same time sums it up:

Therefore the kings of ancient times instituted rituals for wine drinking. With one toast, the host and the guests are obliged to salute each other numerous times. Thus one can drink for the whole day without becoming drunk. This is how the ancients prevented disasters caused by wine drinking. As such wine and food became a means whereby people were brought together in pleasure.

Smother it all in ritual and rite, and everything will be OK. We can have what came to Confucius naturally, drink without drunkenness. The rituals survive in feasting manuals that explain exactly how you should stand and propose a toast to your guests, where everybody should sit, how your wine cup should be on the left side and should not be moved. The etiquette manuals of the period can be very long, and very detailed, precisely because they were seen as the basis of civil order.

So drink, if not banned, was largely restricted to ceremonial occasions. Rituals, funerals, fussy-formal banquets. This meant that if you wanted to get drunk, the method was simple. You turned up at a very formal occasion, and downed everything you could. A later rival of Confucius, a philosopher called Zhuangzi, pointed out that "those who drink following etiquette start off in an orderly fashion but invariably end up in unruliness."

There were complaints about people who went from funeral to funeral trying to get as much alcohol down their throats as they possibly could, presumably while shedding a single, polite tear for the deceased. And there's a whole poem from around the ninth century BC on the subject of

how feasts, no matter how formal, always go wrong. The
first half of the poem is about how the opening of a banquet
is decorous and beautiful and calm and sublime. And then:

> But when the guests have drunk a few,
> Their manner then is something new.
> They leave their seats and roam around;
> They dance and hop and leap and bound. [. . .]
> Yes, when the guests have drunk a few,
> They howl and bawl and shout at you,
> Upset my dishes, spill my food;
> Their dancing gets distinctly lewd.
> For when the guests have drunk a few
> They do not know what crimes they do.
> The cap is toppling off the head,
> The jigging uninhibited.
> If they would leave, they'd have my blessing,
> For drinking's always so distressing. [. . .]
> These drunkards are so sloshed and sleazy
> They make the sober guest uneasy.
> They talk of this and that at random
> And nobody can understand them. [. . .]
> The things you say are not real words,
> Your conversation's quite absurd.
> Three cups, and you make sense no more:
> What happens if you make that four?

Legend has it that at one point in far-off antiquity anybody who had more than five drinks would be executed.
It's certain that when China was united under the Han

Dynasty, a law was passed making it illegal for more than three people to drink together for "no reason." The punishment, though, was a fine, rather than an execution; and the law never stipulates exactly what a good reason would be. Anyhow, it didn't work very well. There was a Han chancellor called Cao Shen who never did any work. Whenever anyone came to complain to him about it, he would offer them a drink, which out of politeness they would have to accept. Then another. Then another. And then they would forget what they had come to say. Then Cao Shen would return to his clerks (who were all pifflicated too) and he would sing to them.

There remains one very curious thing about Chinese drinking. The Chinese did not distinguish between wine and ale. I've used the word *wine* throughout this chapter. But the Chinese word *jiu* could refer to either. This must have meant that, to some extent, the Ancient Chinese just didn't care. This makes them the absolute opposite of the Ancient Greeks and Romans.

CHAPTER 7

THE BIBLE

Noah planted a vineyard. It was the first thing he did after the flood, and to be fair he probably needed a drink. What followed, though, was rather odd.

> When he drank some of its wine, he became drunk and lay uncovered inside his tent. Ham, the father of Canaan, saw his father naked and told his two brothers outside. But Shem and Japheth took a garment and laid it across their shoulders; then they walked in backward and covered their father's naked body. Their faces were turned the other way so that they would not see their father naked.
>
> When Noah awoke from his wine and found out what his youngest son had done to him, he said,
> "Cursed be Canaan!
> The lowest of slaves
> Will he be to his brothers."

This teaches us the important moral lesson that it's absolutely fine to get pass-out-naked pissed, but it is absolutely not all right to notice. You should politely avert your eyes. It's such an eccentric moral that scholars have often felt that we're missing something. Some academics of a suspicious nature have argued that Ham may have done more to his naked father than just look.

This would fit with the next instance of drunkenness in the Bible, a few chapters later, where Lot and his two daughters are living in the mountains. The daughters are worried that they'll never meet nice husbands to get them pregnant, and so they wait till their father is passed out drunk and have sex with him (an unusual solution). But in neither case is it portrayed as the paralytic father's fault. It's just the children being naughty.

To the eternal annoyance of puritans and scolds, the Old Testament is extraordinarily relaxed about the idea of drunkenness. Wine (it is always wine) is just one of those nice things that God gives you, along with grain and oil and peace. Everyone of substance owns a wine press. People drink, they get drunk, and, so long as their children behave, it's all all right. Of course, there's the occasional admonishment against excess boozing. The Book of Proverbs is probably the strictest:

> Who has woe?
> Who has sorrow?
> Who has contentions?
> Who has complaints?
> Who has wounds without cause?
> Who has redness of eyes?
> Those who linger long at the wine,

Those who go in search of mixed wine.
Do not look on the wine when it is red,
When it sparkles in the cup,
When it swirls around smoothly;
At the last it bites like a serpent,
And stings like a viper.
Your eyes will see strange things,
And your heart will utter perverse things.
Yes, you will be like one who lies down in the midst of
    the sea,
Or like one who lies at the top of the mast, saying:
"They have struck me, but I was not hurt;
They have beaten me, but I did not feel it.
When shall I awake, that I may seek another drink?"

It's one of history's most beautiful descriptions of being drunk. It starts as a riddle, turns into a poem and finishes with the comical idea of going to sleep in the rigging of a ship. The Israelites were never sailors, and the sea is always a bit frightening. The whole passage is so lovely that, many, many years later, Andalusian Jews used the words for drinking songs.

A few chapters later, Proverbs gets back to the subject:

It is not for kings, O Lemuel, it is not for kings
    to drink wine; nor for princes strong drink:
Lest they drink, and forget the law, and pervert
    the judgment of any of the afflicted.
Give strong drink unto him that is ready to perish,
    and wine unto those that be of heavy hearts.

Let him drink, and forget his poverty, and remember
his misery no more.

Depending on which translation of the Bible you read,
the "strong drink" that is forbidden to princes sometimes
comes out as "beer," but that's probably wrong. The
Hebrew word is *sheikhar* and it appears to have been a sort
of grappa, or wine made unusually potent. The Israelites
lived in perfect vineyard country, and beer never seems to
have crossed their minds.

Instead, wine is just a commodity, a fact of life and a
comfort to the afflicted. Of the 200-odd references to the
stuff in the Old Testament, almost all are neutral. An
uninteresting but typical example would be this from
Deuteronomy:

He will bless the fruit of your womb, the crops of your
land—your grain, new wine and olive oil—the calves of
your herds and the lambs of your flocks in the land he
swore to your ancestors to give you.

Wine was just another thing you made on your farm.
That's not to say that there wasn't problem drinking in
Ancient Jerusalem. It was familiar enough that it could be
used in similes; and if we put the similes together we can
make a picture of an inebriated Israelite.

They reeled and staggered like drunkards . . . (Psalms)
    They that sit in the gate speak against me; and I was the
song of the drunkards. (Psalms)

The Lord has poured into them a spirit of dizziness;
they make Egypt stagger in all that she does, as a drunkard staggers around in his vomit. (Isaiah)

Then the Lord awoke as from sleep, as a warrior wakes
from the stupor of wine. (Psalms)

Staggering, singing, vomiting, falling asleep—so far,
so familiar. Habakkuk (one of the minor prophets and
a book of the Bible) has a slightly more unusual practice. In describing Egypt's foreign policy in the late
seventh century BC he claims that they've behaved like
a man:

> who gives drink to his neighbors,
>> pouring it from the wineskin till they are drunk,
>> so that he can gaze on their naked bodies!
> You will be filled with shame instead of glory.
>> Now it is your turn! Drink and let your nakedness
>> be exposed!

It does make you wonder. Another detail that suggests
that Judean toping was a little different from ours comes
in the Lamentations of Jeremiah where the prophet
moans and groans about the destruction of Jerusalem and
how there is No More Booze.

> Children and infants faint
>> In the streets of the city.
> They say to their mothers,
>> "Where is bread and wine?"

As they faint like the wounded
In the streets of the city

Which at least suggests that people started drinking at a very young age, although it may simply be poetic license.

Finally, there are no taverns in the Old Testament. Not one. People definitely drank, so we can assume that they did their drinking in the streets, or at home with their nude neighbors.

There was one Jewish group who did not drink. The Nazirites were holy people who had sworn off wine and haircuts. The most famous was Samson, but there was at least one Nazirite in the New Testament.

Drinking and Early Christianity

Drinking in the New Testament revolves around three figures: John the Baptist, Jesus and St. Paul. John made straight the way of the Lord, Jesus brought a new vision to the world and St. Paul was in charge of admin and logistics. I've always felt a little sorry for St. Paul. It's like being in the Catering Corps on D-Day. Terribly necessary, but not that heroic.

John the Baptist was a teetotaler. According to Luke's gospel, his mother had made him a Nazirite before he was born, which seems mean. He certainly fits the description of a Nazirite, out there in the wilderness far away from the nearest tavern or barber.

Jesus was not a Nazirite, whatever some eccentric

theorists may think. Jesus started his career in a shower of booze. The first miracle was the wedding at Cana. It's a simple story. He's at a wedding reception and they run out of plonk. So Jesus turns some water into wine. Roughly 120 gallons of the stuff. The wine is delicious, and the steward of the feast, who doesn't know where it comes from, compliments the host saying:

> Every man at the beginning doth set forth good wine;
> and when men have well drunk, then that which is worse:
> but thou hast kept the good wine until now.

Scholars love to bicker over this line. Some see it as showing exactly how wedding feasts were organized. Some say the opposite.* Some think that the whole story is an allegory, and that the old wine, which has run out, represents the old Jewish faith and that the new wine, which is superior and plentiful, represents Christianity. In the end, it doesn't really matter. What matters to us is that early Christians saw wine as a Good Thing, and an unqualified good. Jesus providing 120 gallons of the stuff is a miracle to be celebrated. There is no suggestion that maybe the guests should all calm down a bit and have an early night. That's significant.

It should be pointed out here that turning water into

---

* For what it's worth, Bultmann and Windisch claim that the best wine was always saved till the end of the wedding feast, and that's what makes the line significant. Sanders disagrees and thinks it's just a joke. Barrett and Lindars are not so sure.

wine was a reasonably well-known miracle in the Ancient world. Dionysus was meant to do it all the time and there are several accounts of springs at his temples that would miraculously run with wine during festivals. We actually know, in one case, how this was done. In the temple of Dionysus at Corinth, there was a secret passage that gave access to the watercourse; so a crafty priest could crawl inside, block the flow of water and pour some wine in instead. That's because, though Jesus was a real god, Dionysus was just pretending. This too will be significant.

Jesus was not going to be another John. In fact, in Matthew, chapter 11, Jesus proclaims quite clearly that:

> For John came neither eating nor drinking, and they say, "He has a demon." The Son of Man came eating and drinking, and they say, "Here is a glutton and a drunkard, a friend of tax collectors and sinners." But wisdom is proved right by her deeds.

So Jesus, in his own lifetime, seems to have had a reputation as a heavy drinker. Whether this was deserved or not is something we shall never know. But it seems interesting that he had to defend himself. And his defense was considered important enough to be included in the gospels (that line pops up in Luke as well). So the early Christians must have thought that they had something to defend.

It may have had something to do with the Last Supper. The central rite of early Christianity was all based around communal drinking, or communion. Jesus drinks wine and commands his followers to drink. This ritual was already around when Paul was scribbling his letter to the Corinthians in the 50s:

> After the same manner also he took the cup, when he had supped, saying, This cup is the new testament in my blood: this do ye, as oft as ye drink it, in remembrance of me.

But the problem that Paul notes in the same chapter is that people were getting drunk at communion. He has to point out that communion is for drinking, not for getting drunk, which must have come as something of a shock to the Corinthians.

Once you start to look for it, you find this problem a lot in early Christianity. The poor apostles were going out preaching the good news of a new religion that required you to drink wine. And people seem to have got the wrong impression. The Acts of the Apostles opens with Pentecost and the Holy Spirit descending upon the Christians, who proceed to speak in tongues. The people in the crowd that gathered:

> asked one another, "What does this mean?" Some, however, made fun of them and said, "They have had too much wine."

And poor St. Peter has to jump up and explain:

> Fellow Jews and all of you who live in Jerusalem, let me explain this to you; listen carefully to what I say. These people are not drunk, as you suppose. It's only nine in the morning!

When you think about it, the drink would have made a perfect stick with which to beat early Christianity. It would be so easy to caricature this strange new sect as a group of drunkards, a Jewish version of the cult of Dionysus, that it would be surprising if pagans didn't do this. That would also explain why Paul, more than anyone else in the Bible, keeps writing letters to people telling them not to get drunk, or to stop getting drunk. Paul was worried about Christianity's reputation.

Mind you, the New Testament never suggests that you should abstain entirely. Instead we are told, "Drink no longer water, but use a little wine for thy stomach's sake and thine often infirmities." Christianity can never be totally teetotal. The Last Supper saw to that. That one sip of wine would change world history, world economics and the drinking habits of far-off lands. Communion requires wine, and so wherever Christianity has spread, the Christians have had to take vines with them. This made the conversion of Yorkshire tricky. Iceland was a nightmare.

CHAPTER 8

THE ROMAN CONVIVIUM

Republic

Early Rome was a very stern and sober place. In the days of the high republic (we're talking about 200 BC–ish), they were all clean-shaven, short-haired militaristic types who were so fond of water that they built huge aqueducts just to keep the eternal city eternally supplied with the stuff. They did have wine, just not a lot of it. And they did have a native Roman wine god called Liber (the free one), but he wasn't terribly important. He was the child of Ceres the wheat goddess and seems to have had some association with free speech. Drunkenness was frowned upon. Sternly. It was associated with the long-haired, bearded, luxurious Greeks, whom the Romans were busy defining themselves against.

The women drank even less than the men. A first-century AD history book called *Memorable Deeds* records this edifying story:

Egnatius Metellus took a cudgel and beat his wife to death because she had drunk some wine. Not only did no one charge him with a crime, but no one even blamed him. Everyone considered this an excellent example of one who had justly paid the penalty for violating the laws of sobriety. Indeed, any woman who immoderately seeks the use of wine closes the door on all virtues and opens it to vices.

Allegedly, Romulus had instituted the death penalty for any woman caught drinking anyway. So Egnatius was just cutting corners. Women were meant to kiss their relatives, simply so that their relatives could sniff them, to tell whether they had been drinking. The early Roman attitude to the whole business can be summed up in one proverb: "Three things are bad: night, women, and wine." All of which helps to explain the peculiar events of 186 BC.

A Greek man (presumably with a luxurious beard) introduced the cult of Dionysus (now called Bacchus) to Italy. Specifically, he revealed the Bacchic mysteries to a bunch of women, who made themselves high priestesses of a secret, new, all-female, all-singing, all-dancing drinking cult, which met at night. These were the Bacchae, or, essentially, maenads.

This seems suspiciously perfect. All the things that the Romans distrusted: night, women, wine and bearded Greeks combined into one. But the Roman authorities certainly believed it, and there probably was *something* going on. Anyway, though it started off as strictly female, which was according to Livy "the source of all the mischief," the priestesses then invited men to join, presumably to liven up the orgies. However, this being a Greek cult, "More uncleanness was wrought by men with men than with women." So now you could add homosexuals to the list of things that virtuous Romans didn't like. They then proceeded to commit all possible crimes:

> When they were heated with wine and the nightly commingling of men and women, those of tender age with their seniors, had extinguished all sense of modesty, debaucheries of every kind commenced; each had pleasures at hand to satisfy the lust he was most prone to. Nor was the mischief confined to the promiscuous intercourse of men and women; false witness, the forging of seals and testaments, and false informations, all proceeded from the same source, as also poisonings and murders of families where the bodies could not even be found for burial.

It all sounds rather fun. But the Senate didn't like it one little bit. It may have been a moral panic. It may all have existed in the senators' fearful imaginations. It may have been a tiny cult whose membership and immorality were exaggerated beyond recognition. But the crackdown was real and stern and brutal.

Rewards were offered for anyone who would inform on cult members. Seven thousand people were arrested. Some fled. Some committed suicide. The majority were executed. The Romans really didn't like drunkenness.

And then they obtained an empire and everything changed.

Empire

The Roman Empire was, in essence, a system whereby the entire wealth of the known world was funneled back to one city. This produced possibly the wealthiest city that the earth has ever known. Money corrupts and huge amounts of money are huge amounts of fun. The result, as every schoolboy learns, was decadence. Roman men started enjoying wine more than water. Then they even let their womenfolk try some. Then they finally read some Greek books and realized they were rather good. And then they thought they'd give homosexuality a go, and that was a big hit. By the time you got to the mid-first century AD those stern senators of 186 BC would have been turning in their graves.

So how did you get in on the fun? The problem with Roman money was that, though there was an awful lot of it, it arrived at the very top of society and flowed down. If you wanted a bit of wealth and wine, you had to find yourself a patron, somebody to sponge off. This sounds horribly parasitical, and in a sense it was, but it was all out in the open. There were patrons with money, and there were dependants with flattery. Everyone knew what was going on. So long as you were prepared to sell your dignity, you got paid in good food and wine. The central component of the system was a banquet called the convivium.

Not everybody liked the system. The poet Juvenal asked: "Is a dinner worth all the insults with which you have to pay for it? Is your hunger so importunate, when it might, with greater dignity, be shivering where you are, and munching dirty scraps of dog's bread?"

And most people said yes.

First, you had to score an invitation. This wasn't actually that difficult. A rich Roman would often give a dinner party every night. The kitchens and the dining rooms were kept in a constant state of readiness. And they did not actually need to know you. Though every patron would have his regular crowd of clients, they would often invite people out of the blue. You might simply be a friend of a friend of a friend. As long as you were presentable and prepared to flatter, you could get an invite in the street.

The Roman day started early. People were up and out of bed at dawn. Hopefully, you had your invitation by midafternoon, which was the standard time to go to the public baths. If you didn't, the public baths were the perfect place to get one at the last minute. You hung around looking amiable, preferably handsome, and tried to strike up a conversation with anybody who looked important. Once you knew that you were going to eat and drink well, the baths were also the perfect place to prepare.

Romans would sit in the sweat room of the bathhouse before a convivium, specifically to try to dehydrate themselves so that they would be ready to drink a lot. This sounds rather weird to us, but it's really no different from our habit of doing a bit of exercise to work up an appetite. According to Pliny the Elder, some Romans didn't even bother with the convivium at all.

Others there are, again, who cannot wait till they have got to the banqueting couch, no, not so much as till they have got their shirt on, but all naked and panting as they are, the instant they leave the bath they seize hold of large vessels filled with wine, to show off, as it were, their mighty powers, and so gulp down the whole of the contents only to vomit them up again the very next moment. This they will repeat, too, a second and even a third time, just as though they had only been begotten for the purpose of wasting wine, and as if that liquor could not be thrown away without having first passed through the human body.

The vomiting is not that unusual either. There's a myth that Romans used to vomit between courses in a special room called the vomitorium. This is untrue. But they often did vomit *before* a convivium, even though they had no special room to do it in.

Going to a Roman convivium would be extraordinarily unpleasant and uncomfortable to any modern drinker. The Greek symposium was all about a meeting of equals. You had a symposiarch, but he was a figurehead. In the end, the Greeks all drank from the same krater. They were men (and only men) together. The Roman convivium was not about being convivial. The Roman convivium was all about showing off, and about asserting who was on the top and who was right down at the bottom. You are not here to have fun. You're here to learn your place, to applaud those above you, and to sneer at those below you.

This was accomplished through seating, slaves, quality of wine, quantity of wine, food, what the wine was served in and where that was thrown. Let's take these in order.

Seating

The dining room contained one big table. One side was left empty as that was the side where the slaves, those endless crowds of slaves, served the brimming platters, and took away the empties. The other three sides had a couch each, and each couch held three people, lying down, because the Romans liked to drink horizontally. Looked at from the slaves' point of view, the couch on the left was for the host and his family, with the host himself farthest from you. The center couch was for important visitors, with the guest of honor on the left, at the corner with the host. The best food and the best wine were reserved for that corner of the table.

The couch on the right was for inferior guests, with the least honored guest nearest to you. That corner of the table, diagonally opposite the host and his friend, could be covered with inferior food and inferior wine for the clearly inferior guest.

If you're there, you weren't really welcome, you certainly weren't honored. The host is telling you that he doesn't give a galley-slave's cuss about you. And you still have to say thank you. That's the point of the convivium. There are even stories of guests being invited purely so that they can be sat in the lowest place and ignored as a form of public humiliation.

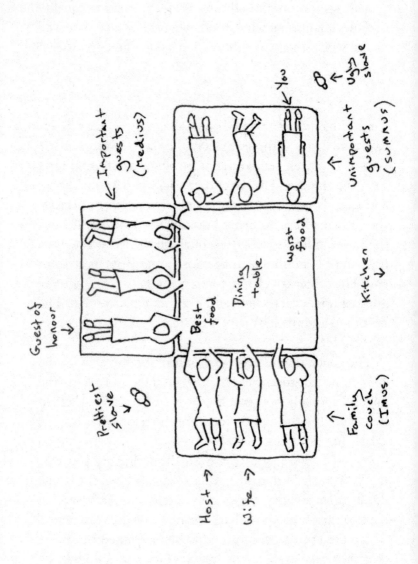

Guest of honour ↓

Prettiest slave ↓

←Important guests (Medius)

Host →

Wife →

Best food

Dining table

Worst food

Family couch (Imus)

Kitchen ↓

You ↓

Ugly slave ↑

← Unimportant guests (summus)

Slaves

The whole house is crawling with crawling slaves. They had to crawl, or they got whipped. Hosts would whip their slaves in front of their guests as a demonstration of power. The longest and clearest description of a convivium we have comes from the *Satyricon* by Petronius. In it the horrifically wealthy, show-off host, vulgar Trimalchio,* is constantly threatening to have his slaves beaten. Half the time it's just a joke, but half the time he's deadly serious. Before the feast has even begun, a slave is blubbing for mercy for having been guilty of some slight negligence. The slave is slavishly grateful and promises to slip them some of the best wine; because, and I know this sounds odd, slaves had some sort of power. An expensive slave would look down on a poor guest.

The Romans' relations with their slaves were, to us, bizarre beyond belief. There was snobbery, there was negotiation, there was love—or at the very least sex, and the latter often turned into an approximation of the former, even when it didn't mean to. There was an awful lot of freeing slaves, individually, on the basis that an intelligent chap was a better business partner than a possession. It was, as I say, odd; but we were in a world where everybody accepted the idea of slavery so long as they were on the right side of it (except the Christians, who were really weird).

* F. Scott Fitzgerald's working title for *The Great Gatsby* was *Trimalchio in West Egg*.

But at the convivium each guest would have his own appointed slave, a personal cupbearer who would serve him and nobody else. So the question was, how good is the slave that's been assigned to you this evening? Romans rated their slaves on looks. The most beautiful, probably Middle Eastern boy would be serving the host. They would then be arranged in decreasing order of good looks for the decreasing importance of the guests. Unimportant guest equaled ugly slave. If you're seat three on the third bench, Juvenal tells us that your drink "will be handed to you by a Gaetulian groom, or by the bony hand of a blackamoor whom you would rather not meet at midnight when driving past the monuments on the hilly Latin Way."

Quality of Wine

The Romans were the original wine-bores. They would go on forever and a day about precisely where the wine they were drinking came from. Which slope, which grape and most importantly which year. In this, the Romans valued age over everything else. The best wine was a hundred years old. It didn't matter whether anyone had tested it, or whether that particular grape actually improved with age. The convivium was not about fun, it was about ostentation. A vintage would be stamped with the name of the consul in power at the time (this changed yearly), but most of the stamps for old wine were probably faked. Finally, the Romans served their wine mixed with hot water that came from a samovar-like device in the corner of the dining room. So actually discerning the ripening notes of Provençal mirth, etc., would be extraordinarily difficult.

That didn't matter because everything here is about rank. And if you're the third guest on the third couch, you don't even get to sip the wine that the host is gulping down. You just get to hear about it. You get a long disquisition on the vintage and provenance of *his* drink, while you are, without disguise or embarrassment, served second-rate plonk. And you have to nod appreciatively.

Wine Cups

The host would be drinking from gold. He might even be drinking from glass. The Roman glass industry had made great strides of late and nobody could quite decide whether it rivaled precious metals. Whichever way you took it, the host was at the top, and you were at the bottom. He had gold but for you, says Juvenal, "no gold is entrusted; or if it is, a watcher is posted over it to count the gems and keep an eye on your sharp fingernails." But you're much more likely to get "a cracked cup with four nozzles."

But don't miss the point of your goblet. The question is how hurlable it is. The convivium would last well into the night, and the Romans had not entirely lost their military mindset. When they got drunk, they got angry; when they got angry, they started throwing their goblets at those they disliked. Cicero's son threw his goblet at Agrippa (because of a complex point of honor). Trimalchio's wife hurled hers at her husband (because he was kissing a slave boy).

This last point leaves us with what ideologues would

have seen as the one semi-redeeming feature of the convivium vs. the symposium: women were allowed. It was a great and momentous time of equality. Seneca himself pointed out that women "keep just as late hours, and drink just as much liquor; they challenge men in wrestling and carousing; they are no less given to vomiting from distended stomachs and to thus discharging all their wine again; nor are they behind the men in gnawing ice, as a relief to their fevered digestions." The convivium does seem to end as it began, with vomiting.

Really, there was nothing to recommend the Roman convivium. It was a vulgar, petty, nasty display of power on the part of the rich, and of parasitism on the part of the poor. Almost every Roman writer pours a goblet of contumely upon it, to the point that it's hard to see why anybody turned up.

There is only one major piece in praise of the convivium. It's by the poet Horace, and he was to be the host. But just so that I can say that I've given both sides of the argument, Horace's convivium does sound all right, even if he lets on in the opening lines that he's only serving a small, *vegetarian* meal. He does go on rather about the particular wines he'll serve (all Romans did), but he also makes his little convivium sound almost pleasant. And the invitation contains one of the few Roman praises of drunkenness:

> Drunkenness works miracles
> Unlocks secrets, hopes fulfills,
> Gives the coward bravery,

Pours away anxiety.
Flowing wine makes verses flow,
And liberates the poor and low.

Horace then promises that the napkins will be clean. He also mentions that the next day is a public holiday, so they can sleep in. A convivium would end after midnight with the guests heading home through the lampless streets of Rome. And then, the next morning, the final stage of Roman drinking was for them, as for us, the hangover. Pliny the Elder gives a good description:

the drunkard never beholds the rising sun, by which his life of drinking is made all the shorter. From wine, too, comes that pallid hue, those drooping eyelids, those sore eyes, those tremulous hands, unable to hold with steadiness the overflowing vessel, condign punishment in the shape of sleep agitated by Furies during the restless night, and, the supreme reward of inebriety, those dreams of monstrous lustfulness and of forbidden delights. Then on the next day there is the breath reeking of the wine-cask, and a nearly total obliviousness of everything, from the annihilation of the powers of the memory. And this, too, is what they call "seizing the moments of life!" whereas, in reality, while other men lose the day that has gone before, the drinker has already lost the one that is to come.

CHAPTER 9

THE DARK AGES

It's a curious thing, but Roman wine got much farther than any Roman soldier ever did. The Roman army entered Germany, got to the Teutoburg Forest, were thoroughly massacred and never went back. But Roman wine entered Germany, got to the Teutoburg Forest and was guzzled down by the thirsty natives who wanted more.

They were a thirsty lot, the natives. If you imagined a bunch of primitive Germans having a low-tech, year-round Oktoberfest, you'd be roughly right.

> To pass an entire day and night in drinking disgraces no one. Their quarrels, as might be expected with intoxicated people, are seldom fought out with mere abuse, but commonly with wounds and bloodshed.

That's according to the Roman historian Tacitus, who also says that the Germans made all of their political decisions while utterly pie-eyed, on the grounds that that made them honest:

Yet it is at their feasts that they generally consult on the reconciliation of enemies, on the forming of matrimonial alliances, on the choice of chiefs, finally even on peace and war, for they think that at no time is the mind more open to simplicity of purpose or more warmed to noble aspirations. A race without either natural or acquired cunning, they disclose their hidden thoughts in the freedom of the festivity. Thus the sentiments of all having been discovered and laid bare, the discussion is renewed on the following day, and from each occasion its own peculiar advantage is derived. They deliberate when they have no power to dissemble; they resolve when error is impossible.

This is, of course, a policy that should be brought into modern politics as it would make TV interviews more fun. It's also the furthest that the principle of *in vino veritas* has been taken. If alcohol makes you speak the truth, and if politics is riddled with lies and liars, wouldn't it make sense to dose them all with booze, the mother of truth? There is a logic to this, just as there is a logic to the Chinese and Indian belief that a ruler should *never* be drunk. Were we to adopt this approach today we would, undoubtedly, have more wars, but we would at least know why.

Tacitus also mentions that, though the Germans made their own beer, they also imported Roman wine. And they drank their Roman wine from golden Roman drinking cups. We know this because the barbarian kings liked to be buried with their most expensive drinking equipment. They believed that they would therefore have it beside them for all eternity to carouse with whatever strange gods they worshipped. They believed wrong, of course, as modern archaeologists keep unsportingly digging them up and separating them.

So when the Roman Empire declined, foundered and fell, the wine trade continued on as best it could, supplying the needs of the vinous Vandal and gambrinous Goth. The problem for us is that these people were so unremittingly barbarian that they didn't write down anything about their drinking customs. We have little glimpses, but the lights go out. These are called the Dark Ages.

One little glimpse we do have is from a Greek chap called Priscus who, in 448 AD, actually had dinner with Attila the Hun. He had been sent to him on a diplomatic mission because Attila was terribly upset that somebody had stolen his precious Roman drinking vessels. He wanted them back, and moreover he wanted to meet the new owner of the drinking vessels, a Roman citizen called Silvanus, and kill him.

So Priscus was sent to smooth things over, with one of the most violent and terrifying men in history; and, after being kept waiting around for a while, was invited to a feast in Attila's biggest and favorite house at three o'clock.

He was taken into a great hall with tables arranged around the walls. Attila's table was in the middle, and Attila's bed was on a platform just behind him. Around the warlord were his immediate family, looking anything other than cheerful. Attila's eldest son was so scared of his father that he just stared at the ground. Then the other guests were arranged in order of seniority stretching out around the room, with the right side of Attila ranking above the left side (in the same way as at a Roman convivium). Priscus was at the last table on the left.

Everyone was given a cup of wine, and after taking one sip from it (the custom) they all sat down in their places. Then the toasts began.

When all were sitting properly in order, a cupbearer came to offer Attila an ivy-wood bowl of wine, which he took and drank a toast to the man first in order of precedence. The man thus honored rose to his feet and it was not right for him to sit down again until Attila had drunk some or all of the wine and had handed the goblet back to the attendant. The guests, taking their own cups, then honored him in the same way, sipping the wine after making the toast. One attendant went round to each man in strict order after Attila's personal cupbearer had gone out. When the second guest and then all the others in their turn had been honored, Attila greeted us in like fashion in our order of seating.

This must have taken ages: a long, formal combination of terror, boredom and being annoyed with the seating plan, much like a modern wedding. Eventually the food came out and everyone fell to eating and drinking and having something like a good time. Except Attila. Attila never laughed. He just sat there with his terrified family watching all his guests eating off silver platters while he ate his dinner from a wooden board.

Then a couple of comedians were brought out, a deranged Scythian and a Moorish dwarf, and everyone was in fits of laughter, except for Attila, who remained nasty, brutish and short. The sun set and torches were lit and eventually Priscus realized that he wasn't going to get any business done that evening and "After spending most of the night at the party, we left, having no wish to pursue the drinking any further."

Priscus returned to Constantinople to write history books, and Attila died of a nosebleed.

Monastic Drinking

The barbarians bounced around Europe in the most distressing manner. They understood that they liked wine, but they didn't have much of an idea of how it was made. Back on the distant steppe they had made a funny drink called *kumis* out of fermented mare's milk. This could be made on the go. When they stopped for a little while, they could make ale from grain. But to make wine you need to carefully cultivate your vineyards for years and years. The barbarians didn't appreciate this. So they would turn up, drink all the wine, burn the vineyards and then get confused when there wasn't any more wine. Then they would ride on, in a very bad mood, to the next town and repeat the process.

It was, in general, a bad time to be an innocent bystander, and a lot of people decided that they really couldn't put up with it anymore. The result, to some extent, was monasteries.

Monasteries were quiet little places away from towns, which were therefore a bit safer. Once the barbarians had been persuaded to become (nominal) Christians, a Christian monastery was (nominally) the safest place to sit back, relax and get stinko.

The trend was started by St. Benedict in the sixth century. He started some monasteries and wrote a book of rules. These were not strict rules, for Benedict was a rather reasonable chap. It's rule number forty that utterly fails to forbid drinking.

> "Everyone has his own gift from God, one in this way and another in that." It is therefore with some misgiving that we regulate the measure of other men's sustenance. Nevertheless, keeping in view the needs of weaker brethren, we believe that a hemina of wine a day is sufficient for each. But those to whom God gives the strength to abstain should know that they will receive a special reward.

A hemina of wine is roughly one modern-sized bottle. Maybe a smidgen under. Now, I know what you're thinking. That can't possibly be enough. What if it's a rather warm day? What if you were thirsty? What if you needed a drink because you'd done something foolish, like physical exercise? Was St. Benedict some kind of monster?

He was not. St. Benedict was a good and thoughtful man who had taken those things into account. The rule continues:

> If the circumstances of the place, or the work, or the heat of summer require a greater measure, the Superior shall

use his judgment in the matter, taking care always that there be no occasion for surfeit or drunkenness.

The choice was between joining a Benedictine monastery and staying at home to be raped and pillaged by every passing Visigoth. It is unsurprising that monasteries flourished. It wasn't that Benedict thought that wine should be compulsory for monks, or even that it was admirable.

We read, it is true, that wine is by no means a drink for monks; but since the monks of our day cannot be persuaded of this, let us at least agree to drink sparingly and not to satiety, because "wine makes even the wise fall away."

Other monastic orders are less clear about the wine ration, but it was clear that wine was available from the rules against drunkenness, harsh rules that punished you for being too sloshed to stand up and sing a psalm. The most extreme penalty was sixty days' fasting, but that was only if you were so drunk that you vomited up the Eucharist. Benedict simply knew that without wine there would be trouble. Rule forty finishes thusly:

But where the circumstances of the place are such that not even the measure prescribed above can be supplied, but much less or none at all, let those who live there bless God and not murmur. Above all things do we give this admonition, that they abstain from murmuring.

And there would be murmuring. The monks of the Dark Ages, indeed the people of the Dark Ages, needed booze because the alternative was water. Water requires a well-maintained well, or preferably an aqueduct, and that requires effective organization and government and all the things that the Dark Ages are not best known for. In the absence of these, your best source of water is the nearest stream, and for most of us, those who don't live high in the mountains, that is a murky prospect.

Water drawn from the nearest stream was barely transparent. It was liable to contain creeping things, whatever they were—worms or leeches. One Anglo-Saxon book recommends a cure for swallowing creeping things: immediately drink some hot sheep's blood. This tells us two things: (a) water was disgusting; (b) people did nonetheless drink it sometimes. Sometimes you had to, you were thirsty and you could afford nothing better. The standard Anglo-Saxon attitude to the subject is summed up in Abbot Aelfric's dictum: "Ale if I have it, water if I have no ale."

Wine, continued Aelfric in a wistful tone, was way too dear for the average English monk. Instead, the standard ration was a mere gallon of ale a day (and more on feast days). Anglo-Saxon monks were as blotto as their Italian cousins. Indeed, when the monastery at Lindisfarne was sacked in 793, a monk called Alcuin wrote the surviving monks a thoughtful letter saying that it was their fault because they had "blurred the words of their prayers through drunkenness," which was probably more true than tactful.

Mind you, Anglo-Saxon England only existed because of booze. The story goes that there was a fifth-century warlord in Kent called Vortigern. He was being attacked by the Picts so he invited two Saxons called Hengist and Horsa to help him defeat them. Hengist brought along his daughter, who was something of a looker, and took her to a feast.

> And after that [Vortigern] had been entertained at a banquet royal, the damsel stepped forth of her chamber bearing a golden cup filled with wine, and coming next the King, bended her knee and spake, saying: "Laverd King, wacht heil!" But he, when he beheld the damsel's face, was all amazed at her beauty and his heart was enkindled of delight. Then he asked of his interpreter what it was that the damsel had said, whereupon the interpreter made answer: "She hath called thee 'Lord King,' and hath greeted thee by wishing thee health. But the answer that thou shouldst make unto her is 'Drinc heil.'" Whereupon Vortigern made answer: "Drinc heil!" and bade the damsel drink. Then he took the cup from her hand and kissed her, and drank; and from that day unto this hath the custom held in Britain that he who drinketh at a feast saith unto another, "Wacht heil!" and he that receiveth the drink after him maketh answer, "Drinc heil!"

Vortigern asked Hengist for his daughter's hand in marriage, and Hengist said yes, on condition that he could have Kent. Vortigern thought this a fair swap, and thus Hengist gained a kingdom and lost only a barmaid.

That is, I'm afraid, only a story, one written up 600 years later by Geoffrey of Monmouth. But it does at least tell us that, in Geoffrey's time, every Englishman, upon being given a drink, would say, "Drinc Heil!"

And it perhaps proves that Tacitus was right about those darkened denizens of northern Europe: "If you indulge their love of drinking by supplying them with as much as they desire, they will be overcome by their own vices as easily as by the arms of an enemy."

The deal between Hengist and Vortigern caused something else. Hengist now had a foothold in Britain. So he sent word back to all his tribesmen and their friends in Denmark telling them to come on over. They came in hordes: the Jutes, the Saxons and, most importantly, the Angles—because that one drink had given them a foothold in this new country that was soon to be called Angle-Land, or England.

CHAPTER 10

DRINKING IN THE MIDDLE EAST

According to the Koran, paradise contains whole rivers of wine. Surah 47:15 is quite specific on the subject:

Is the description of Paradise, which the righteous are promised, wherein are rivers of water unaltered, rivers of milk the taste of which never changes, rivers of wine delicious to those who drink, and rivers of purified honey, in which they will have all [kinds of] fruits and forgiveness from their Lord, like [that of] those who abide eternally in the Fire and are given to drink scalding water that will sever their intestines?

So wine for the blessed, and water for the damned. And, just in case a river of wine isn't enough, Surah 83 of the Koran promises that the good Muslim will also receive sealed flasks of wine so wonderful that even the dregs taste of musk.

This leads to the odd conclusion that a good Muslim will end up drinking more than a good Christian. The latter has a lifetime to drink wine, the former an eternity.

However, the Koran is much less keen on terrestrial drinking. The position actually changes a little, and both scholarship and tradition seem to agree (for once) that the commandments involving wine got stricter as time went by. An early verse would be Surah 16:67 where wine features among the good things provided by God: "And of the products of the palms and the vineyards you take to yourselves therefrom an intoxicant and a fair provision."

When the Koran does remonstrate against drinking, it's pretty mild. There is an injunction not to pray while drunk, which seems reasonable, and also seems to assume that you are drunk a fair amount of the time. Then there is a verse about drinking and gambling that says that "In them is a great sin, and [some] benefit for men, but the sin of them is greater than their benefit." Again, this seems to be reasonably healthy advice.

But then, according to tradition, a fight broke out among Muhammad's followers as a direct result of drinking (one chap threw a lamb's bone at another), and he went back and consulted once more and came up with this:

> O ye who believe! Strong drink and games of chance and idols and divining arrows are only an infamy of Satan's handiwork. Leave it aside in order that ye may succeed.

Most Muslims take this verse as the clincher. Drinking is the work of Satan, and is therefore irredeemably and unchangeably Bad.

After the Koran comes the Hadith, a record of the sayings of Muhammad allegedly collected a hundred or so years later. The Hadith is pretty much completely against wine. It even bans it in medicine and in the manufacture of vinegar. It's in the Hadith that you get the classic punishment of eighty lashes for drinking, and extra prohibitions in a way that makes it look as though people were already looking for loopholes.*

But the Hadith still has that strange view of wine as simultaneously evil and paradisical; it still says: "Who drinks wine in this world without repenting it, shall not drink it in the other world."

But the question for us is, how much *effect* did this all have? After all, the Christian Bible explicitly commands love and forgiveness, to almost no discernible effect. There's a passage in the New Testament where Jesus quite pointedly refuses to endorse the death penalty for a woman taken in adultery. The last woman taken in adultery to be hanged in England was in 1650, under a new law introduced by the Puritans.

Eighth-Century Baghdad

So what did the ban actually do? Initially, not much. There wasn't much wine on the Arabian Peninsula. There

---

* "Allah has cursed Khamr [intoxicants—alcohol, wine etc.], the one who drinks it, the one who pours it for others, the one who sells it, the one who buys it, the one who makes it, the one who it is made for, the one who carries it, the one who it is carried to and the one who consumes the money from its sale." —Sunan Abu Dawud

are a few early references to it being imported for use in monasteries. But desert nomads don't drink much wine. Then, in the seventh century, Islam spread out into Mesopotamia and the Levant, two of the most ancient winemaking regions in the world. And there it changed things a little bit, but not much.

Early Islam was rather tolerant, certainly of Jews and Christians. There was very little conversion at the point of a scimitar. Indeed, the early tactic was to just give tax benefits to Muslims and freedom to everyone else. This meant that if you turned up in eighth-century Baghdad you could easily obtain wine, so long as you went to the Jewish Quarter, or the Armenian Quarter, or the Greek Quarter. There were enough quarters to make a strict mathematician blush.

One chap who went to a lot of quarters was Abu Nuwas. Abu Nuwas is generally considered to have been the greatest Arab poet who ever lived, and his speciality was writing *khamriyyat,* or wine songs. This was a well-known genre of Arabic poetry, which tells you something about how effective the ban was. And the *khamriyyat* of Abu Nuwas give us a pretty good idea of what an evening's drinking (or indeed a dawn-till-dusk session) was like in Baghdad in about 800 A.D.

Nuwas is particularly good because most of his poems follow the same pattern. You start out with your trip to the relevant quarter, "racing each other through the dark alleys" beneath the palace walls. You get to the tavern and you have to bang loudly on the door and shout. The owners were often asleep and, it seems, opened up specially when a big-spending party of Arabs showed up. Nowhere does Nuwas mention other people at the bar besides the tavern keeper, the waiters and the entertainers.

The tavern keeper then asks what they want and Abu Nuwas demands wine. There was quite enough of a market that the keeper would then ask what sort and how much Nuwas and his companions feel like spending. To this Nuwas always replies, "Lots!" and "The best you've got." He's picky about origin, vintage and grapes, and is particularly fond of wine from Fallujah.

The tavern keeper then descends to his musty, dusty cellar and returns lugging a large, sealed flask of wine. This gets Nuwas very excited and he starts to think of the flask as a beautiful girl that he's going to ravish. The tavern keeper inserts a tap and she bleeds "like a virgin." This gets him really, really excited. The wine is poured into beautiful glasses and is usually mixed with ice or cold water. Sometimes Nuwas drinks it straight, but only on special occasions. Nuwas was only straight on special occasions.

This brings us to the other people in the tavern. There was usually a waiter or waitress or singer or flute-player or prostitute or slave. But usually there was a combination of several of the above and this is what gets Nuwas terribly excited. A girl for necessity, but a young boy for preference. Most of Nuwas's nights end up with him sodomizing the waiter, who is always described as handsome, slender and "like a fawn." Nor does Nuwas necessarily get hung up on details like consent, or even consciousness. As for proof of age, it is perhaps best to draw a veil over the proceedings. Not that Nuwas does. He's forever banging on about the "crescent-shaped ravine" or how he rides them like a camel.

An interesting detail of Nuwas's *khamriyyat* is the monasteries. There were a bunch of Christian monasteries just outside Baghdad that clearly did a lucrative side business as speakeasies and, perhaps, rather more. Nuwas and his friends would visit these for all-night sessions.

> The church bell heralds break of day,
> The monk intones his prayer;
> The drunk man longs to have more wine,
> The rain has filled the air.
> [. . .]

> How good it is to have a drink
> In monastery grounds,
> And April is the sweetest month
> To drink in such surrounds.*

Nuwas then sodomizes a choirboy. It's all a trifle unedifying. But that's partially the point. Nuwas likes to line up all the things that you shouldn't officially do, and impishly declare that he did them all. Last night. Twice. Nuwas knows that drinking is illegal, and that's why he loves it so.

In one poem he actually puts a copy of the Koran down

* Translation by Jim Colville from *Poems of Wine and Revelry: The Khamriyyat of Abu Nuwas* (London: Kegan Paul, 2005).

next to his wineglass and comments that one is warm and the other cold. One of Nuwas's main aims was to annoy, to outrage and to get a rise out of the sterner section of the clergy. And it worked. He was thrown in jail and the chief of the Baghdad police apparently made a fortune collecting the bribes from all of his wealthy, degenerate friends who wanted to visit him in his cell.

But Nuwas was only imprisoned briefly, and only because the caliph of the time needed the imams' support in an inconvenient civil war. The moment that was over, Nuwas was out again and drinking with the caliph, who was a good friend of his and a legendary boozehound. It's a point often missed by those who wish to revive the caliphate, that the first time around most of the caliphs were bumpsy.

Nuwas's greatest forerunner, quite possibly the inventor of the *khamriyyat* form, was caliph not long before he was born. Al-Walid II was, if anything, more scandalous than Nuwas, if not quite as good. And he was the *King*. A typical verse of his goes:

> I call upon God to be my witness, as well as pious
>   angels and righteous people,
> That I desire music and song, to drink wine and to
>   bite the cheeks of nubile youths.

When the caliph is writing that, it's unsurprising that the laws become a little lax. It's also unsurprising that the ruler carousing with his courtiers became a stock scene of Arabic literature. There were a lot of merry monarchs. Badis, the great King of Granada, stayed so long in his palace getting smashed that a rumor went round that he had died. Another Spanish ruler, Abbad al-Mutamid, drank himself into one last oblivion as the enemy armies surrounded his city. The history books say of the great Sultan Husayn Mirza Bayqara that "For the nearly forty years that he was King in Khurasan, there was not a day when he did not drink wine after performing the noonday prayer." But they do insist that he never drank with breakfast.

Babur

That last quotation comes from Babur (pronounced *BAH-boor*), who was a terrifying warlord of the sixteenth century. He started out as King of Tajikistan, aged twelve, invaded Afghanistan and northern India and founded the Mughal Empire. He also kept a diary.

Babur's diary is one of the weirdest documents in history. It's personal and unembarrassed and pretty much the sort of diary that you or I might write today. It's filled with little details about the lovely view, or how his friend came to visit, or that he had a terrible tummy-ache. You feel that you know the chap, and that he's a nice chap, and that you'd get along if for some reason a time machine accidentally dropped you down in Kabul 500 years ago. So for January 12, 1519, the entry goes, "Wednesday: we rode out to visit the Bajaur fort. There was a wine party in Khwāja Kalān's house."

Except, and this is a big except, the entry for January 11, the day before, went:

With mind easy about the important affairs of the Bajaur fort, we marched, on Tuesday the 9th of Muḥarram, two miles down the dale of Bajaur and I ordered that a tower of skulls should be set up on the rising ground.

You see, Babur liked to massacre his enemies and build towers out of their skulls. Today you'd call it a trademark, or perhaps a gimmick. But you can never tell with Babur. It's hard to say whether he's a friend manqué or a monster, or maybe both.

Babur didn't drink until he was in his twenties. He'd simply never been interested. But then he did drink, and then he got very interested indeed. And he noted it all down in his diary (along with the massacres and the skull towers and the occasional skinning of his enemies alive). He drank on horseback, in palaces, in boats, on rafts, up mountains and down ravines. Babur loved to booze. Here is a typical example:

November 14, 1519: I told [Tardī Beg] to get wine and other things ready as I had a fancy for a very private party. He went for wine toward Bihzādī. I sent my horse to the valley-bottom with one of his slaves and sat down on the slope behind the kārez [water conduit]. At the first watch [9 a.m.] Tardī Beg brought a pitcher of wine which we drank, just the two of us. After him came Muḥammad-i-qāsim Barlās and Shāh-zāda who had got to know of his fetching the wine, and had followed him, not know-ing I was there. We invited them to the party. Tardī Beg said, "Hul-hul Anīga wishes to drink wine with you." I

said, "I've never seen a woman drink wine; invite her."
We also invited a wandering dervish called Shāhī, and
one of the kārez-men who played the fiddle.

There was drinking till the Evening Prayer on the rising ground behind the kārez; we then went into Tardī
Beg's house and drank by lamplight almost till the Bedtime Prayer. The party was quite relaxed and informal.
I lay down, the others went to another house and drank
there till beat of drum [midnight]. Hul-hul Anīga came
in and wouldn't stop talking; I got rid of her at last by
lying down and pretending to be drunk.

And so Babur meanders on: drinking in the morning,
writing poetry in the afternoon, studiously documenting
the fauna and flora of his domains (he was something of
an amateur naturalist) and slaughtering his enemies and
doing rude things to their corpses.

But this idyllic life could not last. Babur had sworn a
solemn oath to give up drinking when he turned forty. So
when he reached the age of forty-nine (a mere nine years
late) he had all his wineglasses brought to him, and
smashed them up. He even wrote a poem about it.

> I gathered up my golden cups
> And silver ones so fine,
> And there and then I smashed them up
> And freed my soul from wine.

Babur distributed the gold and silver to the poor. And
then he encouraged his courtiers and soldiers to give up

as well. Three hundred leapt on the wagon immediately, and, morally fortified, Babur decided to go and massacre some infidels.

It didn't agree with him, though, teetotalism. He wrote a letter to a friend with the melancholy joke that most people get drunk and then regret it; he gave up drinking and now regrets it terribly. But he couldn't go back and he died three years later leaving the world an empire and a diary.

I should probably spout some guff here about how Babur embodied the paradox of Muslim wine drinking, but that was done much better by his great-grandson Jahangir, who had a wine jug carved with the words *Allahu Akbar*.*

Babur, to do him credit, at least faced up to the dilemma of alcohol in Islam. There is a fine but important distinction to be made. Drinking is forgivable. A Muslim, in most sects, could drink and then repent. But believing that drinking is not a sin, is a sin. So a long procession of sultans cracked down and forgot, or banned and boozed. Pretty much every shah of Persia announced a complete ban on alcohol at some point. But people would just forget about it. There was always a reason. Safi I was crowned in 1629 and immediately banned alcohol, but then he got a cold. It was a very bad cold, and his doctor told him that as it was such a particularly bad cold, he should drink to cure it. Medicinal drinking couldn't possibly be a sin. It was for his health. He died of drink in 1642.

His successor, Shah Abbas II, was crowned and immediately banned alcohol. But he was only nine years old at

* It's rather pretty, and is now in a museum in Portugal.

the time. Aged sixteen he won a battle and that seemed like something of a special occasion, so he had a drink and the special occasion continued until 1666.*

Sultan Husayn made the most serious stab at the business. He was crowned in 1694 and immediately banned alcohol. Six thousand bottles of wine were taken from the royal cellars and publicly emptied in the central square of Isfahan. Sultan was a shah who really, truly meant it. But then his great-aunt told him that she really rather liked alcohol. What's a chap to do? No reasonable fellow can ban something that his great-aunt enjoys. It's coldhearted. So the ban was lifted and soon he and the old girl were merrily drinking away.

Sultan Murad IV (r. 1623–40) had taken a more hands-on approach to the problem of alcohol. He would wander the nighttime streets of Istanbul disguised as a commoner and, with his own hands, kill any Muslim he found drinking. Murad IV was himself a hopeless alcoholic, and any moderately qualified psychoanalyst would Draw Conclusions.

Nothing could stop the shahs and sultans drinking. Their thirst was as unquenchable as their names are unspellable.

Workarounds

However, as the centuries went on and dutifully on, there was a constant nagging from the collective conscience.

---

* Well, actually, he banned alcohol again in 1653, but that ban lasted less than a year.

For a Muslim, drinking is rarely *simple*. The social pressure and the legal bans and, perhaps, the influence of the good old Koran did have their effect. The lower classes found that they rather liked opium, and saw that opium isn't mentioned in the Koran at all, and is therefore OK. The middle classes did become, to some extent, abstinent. But they found loopholes, more loopholes than are contained in the average fishing net.

In Ottoman Bosnia the Muslims were very pious, and did not drink wine. They drank *raki* instead. They argued that, as the Koran never explicitly mentions *raki*, it was all right. That's despite the fact that *raki* is an intoxicating drink made of grapes. One is inclined to think that they were joking, but people took their silly excuses very seriously. A Scottish traveler in nineteenth-century Persia gives this account of an old Sufi whom he met:

> he and some others of tender consciences had contrived
> to provide a means of thus enjoying themselves, without,
> as they chose to believe, transgressing any law. They had
> a spirit distilled from various substances of a saccharine
> nature, with oranges and other fruits; nor do I believe
> that either grain or sugar themselves were quite excluded
> from the composition; and to this they gave the name of
> Mā-ul-Hiāt, an Arabic expression signifying "the water
> of life." It was very strong, and reminded me of whisky,
> highly flavoured with oranges and aromatics. This they
> persuaded themselves was lawful, because it was not
> made from any of the substances expressly prohibited
> by the Mahometan law, and a flask of this spirit was

produced this day after dinner, for the use of Meerza Reza, and others of the more timorous Neophites; it was highly amusing to see Meerza Reza taking the flask in his hand, assume a most puritanical air as he turned to me, and explained the wide difference there was between this valuable liquor of life and that abominable and prohibited trash, called *wine*, and *brandy*, which he never allowed himself (he assured us) to taste. "This," continued he, as he tossed off a well-sized glassful, "is lawful; and very, very good; and I am particularly directed to drink it, on account of a weakness of stomach with which I am distressed."

Human ingenuity can always navigate the labyrinth of religion so long as it is whipped onward by thirst. A German visitor to Istanbul in the sixteenth century described how screaming was meant to momentarily dislodge the soul. Thus the pious Ottoman was able to shriek at the top of his voice, and down as much as he could while his soul wandered confusedly outside his body.* The best ruse, though, was recorded by a Russian engineer of the nineteenth century who was invited to a party given by a wealthy Iranian. Evening prayer was said solemnly. Afterward the host clapped his hands for the servants and ordered them to bring "something and the hats." The servants promptly brought in hats on trays, and the guests, including several mullahs, picked a hat and put it on. That

---

* A technique still practiced at some British bachelorette parties. The traveler, since you ask, was Reinhold Lubenau.

made it fine. They said, "I am not a mullah anymore, but a private person." They immediately started playing board games (which were forbidden), and helped themselves to the "something."

> This "something" consisted of a whole battery of bottles; one could find an excellent cognac, vodka, wine, liquors, and all different kinds of drinks.

So the perfect solution is to put on a hat, scream and drink *raki*. This is, I suspect, true of most of life's problems. Alternatively, you can take the much simpler course of drinking in private. For much of the time during the last few centuries, alcohol has held something like the same place that cocaine does at a party in present-day London. It was consumed quickly and discreetly in a back room. Because of this, drinking could be a peculiarly joyless exercise. Vintage and grape are forgotten; there are neither toasts nor libations; there is no conversation when all you want to do is get the alcohol in you, and get back to the party before anybody has noticed you are gone. It's a question of drinking as much as you possibly can as quickly as you possibly can. This was true of Turks in the sixteenth century:

> They be such people, as openly before any body, they abstaine altogether from drinking of wine: but among themselves privily, all the wine in the world will not satisfie, nor suffice them, such gluttons, & licquorish people they are.

And things had not really changed for the Iranians of the nineteenth century:

> Indeed their maxim is, that there is as much sin in a glass as in a flagon; and that if they incur the penalty, they will not forgo the pleasure; which to them consists, not in the gradual exhilaration produced by wine and conversation among companions who meet to make merry, but in the feelings of intoxication itself; and therefore a Persian prefers brandy, and deep potations, because these soonest enable him to attain that felicity.

And even the theocratic revolution of 1979 didn't dry things out. As one Iranian mullah, Mehdi Daneshmand, put it:

> Not even the Westerners drink alcohol like we do. They pour a neat glass of wine and sip it. We here put a four-liter barrel of vodka on the floor and drink it until we go blind. We don't even know how to drink alcohol or anything. What a bunch we are! We're all the masters of excess and wastage.

And as he said that in the year 2011, I feel we are now up to date.

CHAPTER 11

THE VIKING *SUMBL*

For on wine alone weapon-good
Óðinn always lives.

Odin drank nothing but wine. In fact, he consumed nothing but wine. He didn't eat at all. Nothing to soak up the vino. Not even a cheese canapé. The *Poetic Edda* is quite firm on the point.

It may seem odd that a Scandinavian deity should devote himself to wine, wine not being a well-known Scandinavian product. But that's the point. Wine was the most expensive drink that a rich Viking could buy. It would come up from Germany, or even France, imported from the remnants of the Roman Empire. Wine was a status symbol, and so Odin, top god of the Viking pantheon, pretty much had to have it. The king of the gods could hardly drink ale, it would look bad.

It may also seem odd that Odin didn't eat anything. Wine on an empty stomach is bad for you. Such a regime, continued for all eternity, can cause stomach problems and will almost certainly result in drunkenness. That

Odin only drank wine is probably the reason that his name means, literally, "the frenzied one." Some people translate it as "the ecstatic one," but, to be honest, given his diet, it probably just meant "the drunk one."

This is a reversal. Most polytheistic religions have one chief god, and then a god of drunkenness/wine/brewing, etc., somewhere on the side. Enlil was superior to Ninkasi; Amun to Hathor; Zeus to Dionysus. The drunken god turns up, causes some fun and chaos, but is always subject to the wiser ways and greater powers of the chief god, who usually has a beard. You don't need to be the sharpest theologian to interpret this as drunkenness having to find its niche within society, its little spot where it can be tamed and controlled.

But with the Vikings the chief god is the drunk god. The chief god is actually called "the drunk one." There is no other Viking god of alcohol. It's Odin. That's because alcohol and drunkenness didn't need to find their place *within* Viking society, they were Viking society. Alcohol was authority, alcohol was family, alcohol was wisdom, alcohol was poetry, alcohol was military service and alcohol was fate.

It must have been rather hard to be a teetotal Viking, and no record of such a creature exists.

Now, a little something ought to be said here about the varieties of Viking booze. There were only three. There was wine, as mentioned above, and as mentioned above wine was immensely expensive and almost nobody could get hold of it. The next drink down the pecking order was mead, fermented honey, sweet and reasonably expensive.

Almost everybody almost all the time just drank ale. Their ale was probably slightly stronger than ours at about 8 percent ABV and, according to reconstructions, would have been dark and malty.

But in the Viking sagas all the heroes drink mead, because mead was posher. Similarly, if you wanted to set yourself up as a lord, you needed to build a mead hall, even if all you ever served in it was ale. You still called it a mead hall for appearances' sake. Your mead hall could even be quite small—some were only about 10 feet by 15. Others were huge, a hundred yards in length. In *Beowulf* when Hrothgar wants to become a mighty king, he builds Heorot, the biggest mead hall that anyone has ever seen, filled with pillars and gold.

The mead hall makes you a lord because the very first duty of a lord is to provide booze to his warriors. This was the formal way in which you showed your lordship. And conversely, if you went to somebody's mead hall and drank their mead, you were honor-bound to protect them militarily. Alcohol was, literally, power. It was how you swore people to loyalty. A king without a mead hall would be like a banker with no money or a library with no books.

You also needed a queen, because, strange as it may seem, women were a rather important (if a trifle subjugated) part of the mead hall feast. Women—or peaceweavers as the Vikings called them—were the ones who kept the formal footing of the feast going, who lubricated the rowdy atmosphere and provided a healthy dose of womanly calm. They were in charge of the logistics of the *sumbl*, which was the Norse name for a drunken feast. They may even have enjoyed the beginning of the evening, the first three drinks which were to Odin (for victory), to Njord and Freya (for peace and good harvest), and then the *minnis-öl*, the "memory-ale" to spirits of ancestors and of dead friends.

The first drink of the evening would be served, very formally, by the queen to her husband. She would pour him his mead (or ale) through a little sieve that she kept on a chain around her neck. This was also the point at which she could formally and publicly advise him. This was probably just simple advice like "Drink up," but it was also a chance to make any formal announcement. Once the king had drunk, she would then serve all his warriors in descending order of rank, and finally she would serve the guests.

In fact, serving the drinks was the defining role of women in the Viking age. In poetry you didn't call a woman a woman, you just called her a drink-server. There's a thirteenth-century manual on poetry for the aspiring bard. It lays down that:

> A woman should be referred to in terms of all the types of female attire, gold and precious stones, and ale, wine and other beverages that she pours or serves; likewise in terms of receptacles for ale and all the things that it is fitting for her to do or provide.

So a woman could be called an ale-giver or a mead-maiden or a drinks-dispenser, because to the Viking mind, which wasn't very gentlemanly, that's all she was. The reason for this periphrasis was that Vikings could never call a spade a spade. All Viking poetry was built around the principle of finding an obscure term for a familiar object. So the sea was called "whale's drink" or "the realm of lobsters" or "frothing ale of the shore." Blood was "warm ale of wolves," fire was "destruction of houses" and heaven was "the burden of dwarves." It's what makes Viking poetry so pleasantly incomprehensible.

It's also the reason that you could be drinking your mead out of *hrimkaldar,* or "frost-cups," because the Vikings actually drank from glasses. Not all of them— glass was expensive, but the king in his mead hall would probably have a glass tumbler that looked not much different from the ones that we have today. They came in various shapes, sizes and colors.* Most would look reasonably normal on a table today, if a little kitschy. This is rather disappointing if you imagined all Vikings drinking out of skulls and horns.

There's a funny kind of Viking frost-cup that archaeologists call a funnel glass. That's because archaeologists aren't poets. A funnel glass is about 5 inches tall and is shaped just as you might imagine it, which means that it can't be put down on a table. It would just fall over. This is quite deliberate as the idea is to make you down your whole drink in one. This was immensely important to the Vikings as downing drinks made you a real man. This was also the

---

* For some reason, because the glass is colored, they resemble nothing so much as cheap novelty glasses from the 1970s.

purpose of the more traditional drinking horn: to test your virility by reference to your ability to swallow.

There's a story about Thor (the god of warfare and hammers) and Loki (the god of mischief). Loki challenged Thor to drink a horn of ale. Thor, who could never resist a challenge, accepted and Loki had a horn brought to the table and told Thor that a real man could down it in one. Thor grabbed the horn, put it to his mouth, and drank, and drank, and drank, and, when he could drink no more, the horn was still almost full. Loki looked disappointed and said that a normal chap might need to do it in two. So Thor tried again, and again his godlike drinking had almost no effect. Loki murmured that a weakling could do it in three. Same thing happened. This left Thor feeling rather ashamed and effeminate, until Loki revealed that he had tricked him, and that the other end of the horn was connected to the sea. Thor had drunk so much that he had brought the whole level of the world's oceans down, and that, according to the Vikings, was the origin of tides.

Along with the drinking competitions, Vikings did an awful lot of boasting. This was not seen as a bad thing. A Viking chap was meant to boast. He was meant to recount all of his great rapacious deeds. And then another Viking was meant to outdo him. There were, alas, no modest Vikings, no diffident Norsemen, awkwardly raping and shamefacedly pillaging along the coasts of England. They liked to shout about it, brag about it and say that they'd done more of it than the next fellow.

These boasts were not quick one-liners either. They were long affairs that waxed poetic and lyrical. It was a big, formal occasion, much like a modern rap battle, or so I am informed. Moreover, your boasting was in deadly earnest. You were expected to stand by anything you said, whether it was a claim of something you had done in the past, or of something that you were merely planning on. There was no possibility of excusing yourself the next morning by saying, as we would, that that was just the drink talking. In fact, the reverse was the case. There was a special kind of cup called the *bragarfull*, the promise-cup. If you swore to do something and drank from the *bragarfull*, that promise was utterly and completely binding. There was no way out. The *bragarfull* was fate. Just to make sure that you never went back on a *bragarfull* promise, a sacred boar would be led into the hall and you put your hand on it as you made your oath. The boar was then killed and its spirit would fly off to the goddess Freya and tell her your drunken vow.

There's a story about a chap called Hethin. When the *bragarfull* comes round at the king's feast, he takes it, puts his hand on the boar and accidentally swears that he'll marry his brother's wife. The next day he feels rather awkward about this, as you would, and so he goes and tells his brother what he's done. His brother's reaction is, essentially, "Well, a *bragarfull* is a *bragarfull*, so you're going to have to do it."

> Grieve not, Hethin, | for true shall hold
> The words we both | by the beer have sworn.

Which may tell you even more about the value of women in Viking society. Nonetheless, the brother is killed in an unrelated duel a couple of days later, so it all ends happily.

All of this should go some way to explaining why women were called peace-weavers and why peace-weaving was required. It was a viciously violent society, a hall full of warriors who are being forced to drink much too quickly, ceremonial bragging and insulting, and they're all carrying swords. The result of all this can best be summed up in the Viking/Anglo-Saxon epic *Beowulf*, where the poet is trying to explain just what a wonderful man Beowulf was. He lavishes praise on him, and the highest praise of all is that Beowulf "never killed his friends when he was drunk."

For a Viking, this was clearly something of an achievement—a thing so extraordinary that you'd mention it in a poem.

The Mead of Poetry

Throughout the *sumbl* you'd also have bards and musicians singing away. Poetry was, in the Viking mind, the direct result of alcohol. The story goes that long, long ago there was a war between the gods. In the end they made peace, and to mark the peace they all decided to spit in a kettle. Now, you may be thinking that that's odd and unhygienic, but it should be noted that in many primitive cultures people chew the barley mash and then spit it out in order to start the process of fermenting beer.

Anyway, they then had a kettle full of god-spittle, and out of the bowl popped a chap called Kvasir, who was the wisest man/god ever to be made out of spittle. Kvasir was a generous soul and he wandered the earth teaching mankind all sorts of wisdom until he met two naughty dwarves who killed him and drained his blood into a pot. Then they added some honey to the blood and thus made Othrerir, the mead of poetry.

Then a giant came along and stole the Othrerir from the dwarves and took it off to his mountain palace. Odin heard about this and very much wanted some. But unfortunately the mead of poetry was now in a giant's castle and was guarded day and night by a giant's daughter. Odin, though, had a thirst on him and it's extraordinary what a chap will do for a drink if he really needs one. So he tunneled into the castle and slipped in in the form of a snake.

This only got him as far as the giant's daughter, whom he promptly seduced. Odin promised to marry her if she gave him a drink of the mead. This may refer to the occasional custom in the Viking world that if a girl gave you a special drink, you had to marry her. It's unclear how widespread this was as most marriages were simply arranged, but it's another example of how accepting a drink could make you kinsman/warrior/husband of whoever provided it.

Odin, though, was a cad. He downed the whole thing in one (typical), turned himself into an eagle and flew off with the mead of poetry in his stomach. The giant saw this and promptly turned himself into an eagle and set off in hot eagly pursuit.

It was a very close-run thing. When the other gods caught sight of Odin returning to their home of Asgard, they put out a vat for him to vomit the Othrerir into. The giant nearly caught up. Odin dived down and puked up pure poetry into the vat. In fact, he was so eager and so bursting with poetic fervor that some of the mead of poetry shot out of his arse. The mead that he vomited up into the vat is responsible for all the great human poets who have ever lived. The stuff that came out of his arse is responsible for the bad poetry. One myth thus explains both Shakespeare and Joyce Kilmer.

Ale

Everything in Viking life centered on ale. People sacrificed the stuff to Odin. People lived for it, poets were inspired by it and warriors killed for it. In one of the heroic sagas a king decides to settle the jealousy between his two wives by keeping the one who, when he returned from battle, gave him the best ale.

By the end of the night the mead hall was probably rather a messy place. Only a couple of things are missing. Two of the usual outcomes of intense drinking are vomit and sex (for preference not simultaneously). For an Ancient Egyptian these would be the whole point. But the Vikings never mention either, despite all their drinking horns.* Instead they dozed off.

There's a lovely mythical creature called the Heron of Oblivion (I've no idea why) that was said to come down and hover over the *sumbl* until everybody dozed off. Nobody went home. You stayed in your lord's mead hall until you could stay awake no longer and then you lay

* Odin's regurgitation seems to be more like that of a mother bird feeding her chicks than that of a lady at an Egyptian banquet.

down on a bench or a table or whatever you could find and you fell fast asleep.

This was a slightly dangerous moment. All the warriors are passed out drunk and unable to defend themselves. The poem *Beowulf* is all about how a monster creeps into the mead hall at night and eats people, until the hero has the clever idea of staying halfway sober.

To be fair, the risk of being eaten by a monster was statistically negligible, but you might be incinerated. There was, apparently, an eighth-century Swedish king called Ingjald who invited all the neighboring kings to his coronation. When the *bragarfull* came round, he swore to enlarge his kingdom by half in every direction. Everyone drank. Everyone got drunk. The Heron of Oblivion did his restful work, and when everyone else was asleep, Ingjald went outside, locked the doors and burned down his own mead hall with all the other kings in it.

I'd like to say that that was a one-off, but it wasn't. There are a fair few accounts of burning down mead halls with everyone in them. There's even one of a queen doing it to her husband, which seems fair.

But being dead wasn't so bad if you were a Viking. They rather looked forward to it. Death simply took you off to Valhalla, and Valhalla was a perpetual party, a *sumbl* that lasted into all eternity. There was Odin, frenzied on wine, there were all the old friends to whom you had drunk your memory-ales, and there was Heidrun, the sacred she-goat whose udders eternally spurt forth good, strong mead. That was the Viking paradise, and in Valhalla you were drunk forever.

CHAPTER 12

THE MEDIEVAL ALEHOUSE

We all have an idea of what a medieval tavern was like. Lord alone knows where we got it from. Perhaps it was a film about Robin Hood and his Merrie Men in the time of Good King Richard, sneaking out of Sherwood Forest and into a village inn. Here rosy-cheeked rustics gathered round the bar swigging from foaming tankards of True Englyshe Ale served by a buxom barmaid. Those with a slightly fruitier imagination may increase the buxomness of the barmaid and the merriness of the men. There was a fiddler in the corner, and, outside, the neatly painted sign swings in the night breeze.

None of this existed.

To explain why, I'll need to explain some bits of nomenclature that I quite deliberately messed up in the first paragraph. These days, one can open a bar and call it the Ship Inn, or the Ship Tavern or just the Ship, and nobody notices or cares. But to medieval people, and all the way up to the late eighteenth century, there was a clearer-than-crystal distinction between an inn, a tavern and an alehouse.

Inns

An inn was a hotel, and a rather expensive one at that. By definition it had lodging and stables for all your horses. When a nobleman went traveling, he stayed at an inn. So did a merchant, or anybody of means. Poor people were rarely allowed through the door. This was partly to keep the tone up, and partly because inns had an unusual pricing structure. A room was actually quite cheap, and the innkeeper made money by charging for all the extras: fine dining, wine, laundry, stabling and the like.

There was no such thing as a village inn, any more than you might expect to find a village Grand Hotel. Only a big town, or more usually a city, would have an inn. It would be a substantial building on the market square, usually built around a big courtyard. Sessions of court might be held in an inn and that, frankly, would be the only way that Robin Hood might be found there.

At the edge of London, the inns were a little shabbier. That's because the gates of London were closed at dusk, and travelers who arrived later than that were forced to stay the night just outside the city walls. Enthusiastic teachers will sometimes tell you that English literature begins in a pub, because the opening scene of *The Canterbury Tales* is set in the Tabard just south of London Bridge. But the Tabard was not a pub, it was an inn. In fact, it was the sort of inn that could accommodate twenty-nine pilgrims and their horses at short notice; and as Chaucer points out, "The chambers and the stables weren wide,/

And well we weren eased at the best." Chaucer's host was Harry Bailey, who was the real-life owner of the Tabard. Many people deduce from this that he was a sort of friendly barman figure. He was not. Harry Bailey was an innkeeper. That meant that he was a very wealthy businessman. He was also an MP, and the collector of the newfangled poll tax.

English literature does not begin in a pub, it begins in a hotel.

Taverns

Taverns sold wine. Wine, because it had to be imported, was very, very expensive. A tavern is roughly the social equivalent of a cocktail bar today; and there is no such thing as a village cocktail bar.

Taverns were for wealthy men who wanted to splash a bit of cash, which meant that they were almost all in London. It also meant that taverns could have a rather degenerate side. This is where you'd find prostitutes and gamblers because, by definition, if you could afford wine you could afford other sinful luxuries.

We have a complete and beautiful portrait of the Tudor tavern in Shakespeare because the Boar's Head Tavern in East Cheap is where Falstaff spends most of his time and all of his money. People often get Falstaff wrong. They think that he and his companions are the poorest of the poor and the lowest of the low. But Falstaff drinks sack—or sherry as we would call it now—and sack, which had to be imported from Portugal, was the most expensive drink available in Tudor England. The modern equivalent would be a man who insisted on drinking only champagne. Certainly, Mistress Quickly's establishment is sleazy, but it's not cheap. At one point Shakespeare reveals that Falstaff has spent about six shillings on sack in a typical day, which was about two or three times what a manual laborer would make in a week. To push the analogy further, a modern Falstaff might be swigging his champagne in a gaudy lap-dancing bar.

Shakespeare, I'm pretty sure, was a wine-drinker. His works have over a hundred references to wine and sack, and only sixteen to ale. It's also the *way* that he thought: when he's searching for a metaphor he talks about the "dregs of life"—stuff like that. In Shakespeare, the suggestion that somebody drinks ale is usually an insult. This fits with the very little we know about Shakespeare's drinking habits. We know for certain that he drank in the Tabard Inn because he carved his name in the woodwork, and there's a good chance he also visited the Mermaid Tavern and the Golden Cross in Oxford. But he seems to have kept things posh.

It's a shame, because we like to think of our literary lions as friendly folk who toddled down the pub with the rest of us. An awful lot of pubs today have a sign up with a quotation from Dr. Johnson: "There is nothing which has yet been contrived by man, by which so much happiness is produced as by a good tavern or inn."

We know exactly what Dr. Johnson meant by that, because Dr. Johnson wrote a dictionary in which he still insisted on the definitions I've given above. Dr. Johnson was quite explicitly excluding the third kind of drinking establishment, the forerunner of the modern pub: the alehouse.

Alehouses

So, with all that in mind, let us return to Robin Hood and his Merrie Men arriving at the village *alehouse* in the time of Richard the Lionheart.

It still didn't exist.

In England in the year 1200 there was no such thing as a pub. Villages simply did not have drinking establishments. This may seem strange. Imagining England without a village pub is like imagining Russia with no vodka (there was, at this time, no vodka in Russia; but we'll come to that in another chapter). There were no pubs, because there was no need for pubs.

It's a funny thing, but the more you think about it, the harder it is to see the purpose of a pub. You might say that it's a place to drink, but you can drink anywhere. And medieval people did drink just about anywhere and everywhere. They drank at work. As usual there were the monks, like the ones at Beaulieu Abbey who were given a ration of one gallon of ale a day. But everybody was drinking at work. Often it was part of the pay. A carter, for example, might expect to have 3 pints and some food thrown in with his wages. When a lord employed laborers to work his land, he had to give them some booze. That's how life worked. Not that people got drunk. A few pints spread out over the course of a hard day's toil in the fields won't do that. But it will nourish you. Ale is, after all, liquid bread.

People drank in church as well. The medieval village church was not so much a place of worship as a community center (with some worship thrown in on Sundays). People would play football in the churchyard and sing songs in the hall. Ale would often be handed out at feast days, name days, weddings, baptisms and funerals. A good funeral could be a pile of fun. When they buried the Bishop of Winchester in 1319 a thousand gallons of ale were given out to the poor. That was an extreme case, but opportunities to cadge booze in church were neither few nor far between.

And most of all, medieval Englishmen drank at home. So did medieval Englishwomen and medieval English children. Water was still pretty dangerous, and only for the very poor. The rule of Aelfric, mentioned a couple of chapters ago, still held: "Ale if I have it, water if I have no ale." And pretty much everyone had ale. Making ale was a simple process that basically involved barley and water and some spices if you had them. So while a man was out working in the fields his wife would be brewing away.

Brewing was always women's work, just as it had been in Ancient Mesopotamia. A husband would expect his wife to cook and clean and look after children, and brew, and spin. Spinning wool into cloth and brewing ale had the added advantage that they could make you extra money. A wife would weave the cloth to clothe her husband, and, if there was any left over, she could sell it. This was almost the only way that the average medieval single woman could get an income. And it was so common that an unmarried woman is, to this day, called a spinster. Note that -*ster*, in this context, is the female suffix; a man who spun would be called a spinner. But men didn't spin. Similarly a woman who brewed would be called a brewster, and the name survives.*

A woman who brewed for profit could also be called an alewife. Medieval ale had a very short shelf life. It would go off after two or three days. So when an alewife had brewed more than her family needed, she would put up an ale stake above her front door. This was just a horizontal stick with a sprig of bush tied to the end. She would put the barrel outside her house, and sell to passersby who would turn up with a flagon and some pennies. They could then stroll off and drink it at work, at their own home or in church. When the excess ale was all sold, the alewife took the ale stake down and began brewing some more.

That's how things were all the way up to the beginning of the fourteenth century. Then several things happened at once. First, people stopped drinking in churches. This was not because they didn't like drinking in church, but because the church didn't like people drinking in it. Simon Langham was made Archbishop of Canterbury in 1366 and the first thing he did was to threaten to excommunicate anybody

---

* Oddly enough, in modern English, where we've forgotten that -*ster* is female, the -*sters* are all semi-criminal: gangsters, mobsters, hipsters, and pollsters.

attending "these common drinking bouts which by a change of name they call charity scot-ales."

Second, there was a change in the way that land was farmed. Once upon a time, a nobleman employed people to till his fields. But in the fourteenth century noblemen decided that it was simpler just to rent plots of land out to the peasants and let them farm it for themselves. This meant that any peasant who didn't have a good alewife now had to go and buy ale, which was good news for ale-wives. Thirsty laborers would show up *after* work, they wanted ale, but they also wanted somewhere to sit down and drink it. So alewives started to let people into their kitchens. Thus the pub was born.

Finally, beer was invented. Throughout this chapter I've been talking about ale, which was made with barley and water. It was not a very pleasant substance. Nutritious? Yes. Alcoholic? Yes. Tasty and pure and fizzy and refreshing? No. It was a sort of sludgy porridge with bits in it. The only way to make it taste nice was to flavor it with herbs and spices—horseradish was a favorite. But you were trying to disguise the taste. Trying to make something vile into something drinkable.

Then hops arrived. Hops are the seed cones of the hop plant and when you add them to ale you get beer. The Europeans had been doing this for ages, but the English were behind the times. Hops first arrived in London and then spread, slowly, over the whole of England. There were some holdouts. In Lancashire they were still drinking ale up to the mid-seventeenth century, and Cornwall kept at it for a long time. Somebody wrote a poem about it:

Ich am a Cornishman, ale I can brew
It will make one to cack, also to spew,
It is thick and smoky and also it is thin,
It is like wash as pigs had wrestled therein.

Most people much preferred the taste of hoppy beer. And beer had one other massive advantage over ale: it didn't go off. You could keep beer for a year or so and, as long as the barrel was well sealed, it would still be good.

Because of this, beer could be mass-produced. In every major town, breweries were set up which could produce lots of lovely beer that could then be sold to all the local alehouses (they continued to be called alehouses, long after the awful sludgy porridge had been forgotten). The breweries could filter the beer and make a much better product. They were also owned and staffed by men. The alewives might have been out of a job, but they weren't because they continued to run their little alehouses, and simply bought the beer in.

A Trip to the Pub

So let us suppose that we are travelers sometime around the end of the fifteenth century. We're thirsty and we stop off in a village to have a pint. What's it like?

Well, first of all we need to find the alehouse. This is still marked with an ale stake. Pub signs (and by extension pub names) don't come in until the 1590s. Inns had had names and signs for centuries, and because inns were posh, pubs tried to emulate them. But for the moment we're just looking for the horizontal stake above the front door with a bit of bush tied to the end. Another marker will be the ale bench, which, as you may have guessed, was a bench just outside the door where, in fine weather, you could sit and drink in the sunshine. It's also quite possible that we'll spot some people playing games—bowls was a favorite—and betting on them.

The door will be open. This was a legal requirement,* except in the depths of winter. The idea was that any passing authority figure should be able to see inside an alehouse and thus check that nothing naughty was going on, while also not having to sully themselves by actually going in. It must have made the place rather drafty, but cold and drafts were near-universal facts of medieval life. This was, after all, a time before glass windows were common. The cold was everywhere, and indeed one of the great advantages of visiting an alehouse was that there was usually a fire blazing away. Many medieval peasants simply couldn't afford such a luxury in their own homes.

One of the first differences we'll notice from a modern pub is that there is no bar. Countertop bars, the sort of thing we know and love, don't actually come in until the 1820s. This place doesn't *look* like a pub. It looks like somebody's kitchen, which is basically what it is. There's a barrel of beer somewhere in the room. And there are a few stools and benches, perhaps a trestle table or two. But

---

* There were no national laws about alehouses until the mid-sixteenth century. But most local magistrates applied roughly the same rules.

the total value of the furniture isn't more than a few shillings. We are in somebody's house, but it's public.

The person whose house we're in is almost certainly a woman. Whether she's brewing her ale on site or buying her beer, this is overwhelmingly a female profession. She may, of course, be married, in which case her husband is legally the owner of the alehouse. But he would still be out doing his normal job, while his wife provided the family with a second income. There's also a good chance that she's a widow. Running an alehouse was still one of the only ways that a woman could make money, and, in the days before pensions, alehouse licenses would be granted to widows out of pity. It was that or she would have to throw herself upon the parish, which the parish found inconvenient.

As we walk in, the room does not fall silent. Travelers were very much expected in alehouses—that was half the point of them. People applying for alehouse licenses would often point out that there were thirsty travelers on the road and not enough alehouses in the area to supply them all.

We actually know a fair amount about who was in the alehouse. Crime is a wonderful thing, if you're a historian, because whenever a crime came to court the names of all the witnesses would be presented along with their trade and their hometown. This means that when a crime was committed in an alehouse, a little record was left. This produces some mathematical oddities. For example, there are about ten guests in there, of whom 5 percent are female.

In fact, women usually went to alehouses in groups. A woman on her own might be talked about. A group of respectable matrons, though, was in the clear. People also went on dates to alehouses. If a couple were known to be courting, then going out for drink was considered perfectly normal and respectable.

Respectable, there, is a relative term. Alehouses were only for the poorest in society. Even moderately well-off people like yeoman farmers were still drinking at home. The alehouse was a place of escape. Servants came here for the same reason as lovers; it was what anthropologists call the Third Place. It wasn't work, where you have to obey your boss, and it wasn't home, where you have to obey your parents or your spouse. That's also why the place is full of teenagers. Medieval England was an edenic place where there were absolutely no laws about underage drinking.

Not that people will actually get that drunk, unless it's a Sunday. Just as we think of Friday night as the standard time for drinking, the medievals liked to get sloshed on a Sunday morning. This makes a lot of sense, if you think about it, as you get to be buzzed all day. But it does mean that there is a permanent war between the alehouse and the church for attendance on a Sunday morning. A war that the alehouse tended to win. There's a story from Staffordshire about an angry vicar trying to get the poor out of their alehouse. The end result was the priest being chased by a mob "flinging his hat into the sky, whooping and crying, begone vicar with thy knapsack."

So we sit down. The hostess pours us a drink in an earthenware vessel. This is often stained black inside; but don't worry, that's just so that she can cheat us on the measures (another point that goes back all the way to Ancient

Mesopotamia). And then we chat. The standard greeting for a stranger arriving in an alehouse was "What news?" In the days before newspapers and even television, travelers were the main way to find out what was going on in the world. Who was king? Were we at war? Had we been invaded? Alehouses actually developed a rather bad reputation for spreading absolute lies. In 1619 the whole of Kent was sent into a panic by the news that the Spanish had taken Dover Castle; and, very curiously, the alehouse drinkers of Leicester heard the news of Elizabeth I's death forty-eight hours before it happened.

So we chat and we drink. Three pints was about standard for a session, except on Sundays. We play games and we gamble. We run up a bill that we will pay at the end of the session. If we're locals we can go for whole weeks buying on credit. Otherwise we can always pay with a sort of barter. You could hand over just about anything in exchange for a pint—a chicken for example. This was convenient, but rather problematic from a criminal point of view. All a traveler had to do was steal a chicken as he traveled and then exchange it for beer at the next alehouse.

And when the evening comes to its end, as all evenings do, and the locals toddle off to their local homes, we can, for a price, fall asleep on one of the benches. Or, for a higher price, we may be able to share a bed with the landlord and his wife. Or we can take our cue from Shakespeare and the only scene he ever set at an alehouse, the opening of *The Taming of the Shrew*, where Mr. Sly is thrown out because he can't pay for his beer, and falls asleep in the street outside.

143

CHAPTER 13

THE AZTECS

We know the Aztecs had booze, and we know that they hated it, and we know that they drank it. After that things become a little confused.

The Aztecs had *pulque*,* which is a funny, white, rather viscous drink about as strong as beer or cider. It's made out of the fermented sap of the agave plant, and it's actually rather good for you. It has vitamins in it and potassium and whatnot. It's full of nutrients and an old saying says that *pulque* is only just short of being meat. It's therefore not that surprising that pregnant women were *meant* to drink it. They were drinking for two.

But *pulque* was frowned upon by the Aztecs. A new emperor, on his coronation, issued a proclamation declaring that:

> What I principally command is that you shun drunkenness, that you do not drink *pulque*, because it is like

---

* The Nahuatl word was *octli*, and the Spanish sometimes referred to it as the natives' wine. I've used *pulque* throughout to avoid confusion.

henbane which removes man from his reason . . . This *pulque* and drunkenness is the cause of all discord and dissension, and of all revolts and unrest among the towns and kingdoms; it is like a whirlwind that upsets and disturbs everything; it is like an infernal storm that brings with it all possible evils. Before adultery, rape, debauching of girls, incest, theft, crime, cursing and bearing false-witness, murmuring, calumny, riots and brawling, there is always drunkenness. All those things are caused by *pulque* and by drunkenness.

This is not exactly an endorsement, but it does suggest that *pulque*-drinking and *pulque*-drunkenness were widespread. And that's really odd, because according to the same historian *pulque* was practically illegal.

One of the problems with writing any sort of history about the Aztecs is that there's very little of it written down. The Aztecs did have their own writing system, but when the Spanish arrived they helpfully burned any native texts they could lay their hands on. Once the culture had been thoroughly smashed and the writings burned, the Spanish decided that it was worth investigating. The main investigator was a priest called Bernardino de Sahagún, who recorded the imperial proclamation above. But he also recorded that:

Nobody drank *pulque* excepting only those who were already aged, and they drank a little in secret, without becoming drunk. If a drunk man showed himself in public or if he were caught drinking, or if he were found

speechless in the street, or if he wandered about singing
or in the company of other drunkards, he was punished,
if he were a plebeian, by being beaten to death, or else he
was strangled before the young men (of the district) by
way of an example and to make them shun drunkenness.
If the drunkard were noble, he was strangled in private.

I don't know what comfort privacy is when you're being
strangled, but I suppose it was something. One might
imagine that Sahagún was exaggerating here, but he almost certainly wasn't. The Aztecs were an extraordinarily
bloodthirsty bunch who had an enthusiasm for human
sacrifice that we would consider unhealthy. Adultery had
roughly the same punishment system of death for all
instances no matter what your social position. Male
adulterers had their heads smashed open with a stone,
female adulterers were strangled and then had their heads
smashed open with a stone. Moreover, we know the laws
on drunkenness in another Mexican city. Texcoco was to
the northeast of the main Aztec city of Tenochtitlan. It
was ruled for a while by an eccentric chap called Neza-
hualcoyotl who built a temple to an unknowable god, which
was completely empty. He issued laws about drinking.
The punishment for a priest who drank was death. For
a government official it was death (unless there was no
scandal attached, in which case it was simply loss of
his job and titles and everything else). A plebeian who
drank actually got off on the first offense. Well, by "got
off" I mean he had his head shaved in public while the
crowd jeered at him. But he wasn't actually hanged. That

happened only on the second offense. This makes Neza-hualcoyotl rather lenient, relatively speaking.

But if drinking was so very, very illegal, how did it have such a central place in Aztec culture? And it did. They had gods of drinking. Several of them. Mayahuel, who was the goddess of the agave plant, was said to have married Patecatl, who was the god of fermentation. Mayahuel had 400 breasts, which was probably fun for Patecatl, but was also useful because she gave birth to 400 divine little rabbits, the Centzon Totochtin.

The reason that there were 400 of them is that the Aztecs counted in base twenty. Four hundred is twenty squared and so the number had much the same place in their culture that 100 (ten squared) does in ours. The reason that they were rabbits is unknown. It may be that rabbits are senseless, or it may be that they're licentious, or it may be that they are just cute. But the rabbits were important in Aztec religion and their priests ranked very highly. They weren't some minor, forgotten-about gods, they were central.

But the thing that they represented was forbidden on pain of death.

Except that here we again have to take into account a contradiction, and again this isn't my fault, it's the fault of the conquistadors who decided to destroy a culture before recording it properly. Alcohol was legal for old people. Nobody is quite sure how old you had to be, but so far as one can tell, you had to be old and wrinkled and retired from everyday life. Once you were no longer useful as a laborer, you could get as drunk as you fancied.

Sahagún, the *same* historian who described all those horrific penalties, also describes an Aztec naming ceremony (essentially a baptism) thusly:

> At night the old men and old women gathered to drink *pulque* and to get drunk. In order that they should get drunk, a large jar of *pulque* was put before them, and the person who served it poured the drink into calabashes (squash) and gave each one a drink in turn . . . And the server, when he saw that the guests were not yet drunk, began serving them again in the reverse order, beginning at the left side by the lower end. Once they were drunk, they would sing . . . some did not sing, but held forth, laughing and making jokes; and when they heard anything funny they would roar with laughter.

So, to recap, booze is ferociously forbidden and punishable by death. Booze is ubiquitous. Booze is revered and central to the culture and religion. Booze is legal for the elderly. This combination has left historians somewhat confused, and indeed inclined toward a quick dose of *teonanacatl*, the Aztec hallucinogen of choice that was entirely legal.*

There is, though, a theory that makes sense of all this. Anthropologists who study drunkenness draw a distinction

---

* Even this one's pretty confusing, though. *Teonanacatl* was apparently taken immediately before a meal, and sent you on a trip that lasted hours and induced vomiting, which can't have done much good for the napkins.

between what they call "wet cultures" and "dry cultures." In wet cultures people are terribly relaxed about alcohol. They sip it all day and have a terribly pleasant time, and very rarely get properly, falling-over drunk.

Dry cultures are the opposite. They aren't dry in the sense of being alcohol-free; they're called dry because people are very wary of alcohol and have strict rules about when you can't drink it. Then, when it is permitted, they get trollied.

Typically, southern European cultures are wet. An Italian will think nothing of sipping a little limoncello at noon on a weekday. North European cultures are dry insofar as they involve no booze in the mornings, and then a massive session on Friday night. Hence, these two are sometimes referred to as "continental-style drinking" and "binge-drinking."

The Spanish conquistadors were, even then, wets. They liked their wine and they sipped it all day, but they rarely actually got sloshed. The Aztecs, by this theory, were dry. On most days, they weren't allowed to touch the stuff, and that's when all those laws listed above were applied. But on the day of a religious festival—for example, one devoted to the 400 drunken rabbits—they got absolutely hammered. They got apocalyptically and religiously drunk, and, like the Ancient Egyptians and the Ancient Chinese before them, they used alcohol to give them an experience of the divine.

And then for the rest of the month they didn't drink at all.

This system could have worked very well, providing

that nobody came along, conquered you and destroyed your religious calendar—which is precisely what happened to the Aztecs. A dry culture can get along just fine, with binge-drinking Fridays and sober Mondays, but somebody *has* to know what day of the week it is. And by the time that the Jesuits were through with them, this vital knowledge had been lost.

At that point, alcoholism becomes pandemic, which is exactly what happened in Spanish Mexico. Indeed, the Catholic priests had a theory that Satan was driving the natives to dipsomania because he wanted to stop them becoming good Christians. By this theory, though, it was precisely the opposite. It was the relaxation of the rules and the disorientation of society produced by Christianity which pushed the conquered to perpetual *pulque*.

This would fit with what little we know about other pre-Columbian Amerindian boozers—not that we know much, and the little we know is scattered over many thousands of miles. But, for example, the people of Zumbagua in Ecuador drink in order to communicate with ancestral spirits, and, indeed, believe that when you drink so much that you throw up, the vomit becomes food for the ghosts of the dead.

And the old culture was never fully and completely destroyed. To this day there is a phrase in Mexico: "As drunk as 400 rabbits."

CHAPTER 14

THE GIN CRAZE

Madam Geneva

Madam Geneva has absolutely nothing to do with the city of Geneva. She was instead the British goddess of gin, which makes her a lot more interesting than anything in Switzerland. Her name comes, ultimately, from the Old French word *genevre*, which means juniper. This got taken into Dutch as *jenever*, which also meant juniper, or could mean the clear alcoholic spirit in which juniper is the main flavoring—the thing we'd now call gin.

Very few pictures of this curious lady survive. This is odd because, in her day, she was quite the celebrity. Poets wrote plays and poems in honor of this great lady, with catchy titles like *Mother Gin: A Tragi-Comical Eclogue* (1737); and her funeral was held in front of huge crowds, several times. She was a socialite and feminist hero "held in the highest Esteem by those of her own Sex, even of the first Quality, being admitted into their most *private Apartments*, ever *at hand* to administer Relief under the many

Disappointments and Afflictions, so unfortunately incident to that tender Part of Creation" (i.e., women).

This is quite something for a goddess of "very mean and obscure Birth, insomuch that she was frequently reproached by those that were no Friends to her, with being sprung from the Dunghill, an Expression generally used to denote a Person of low Rank and Parentage." That at least is the pedigree we have in *The Life of Mother Gin; containing, A True and Faithful Relation of her Conduct and Politicks* (1736). But in fact, her family goes back an awfully long way.

History of Spirits

The history of spirits is a very vexed affair, but it's worthwhile having a quick summary here. There are a bunch of questions that should be answered:

1. When was distilling invented?
2. When did people distill *alcohol*?
3. When did people have the idea of drinking distilled alcohol?
4. When did people start mass-producing distilled alcohol so that common drunkards could get their hands on it?

The rough answer is that the Ancient Greeks definitely knew about distilling over 2,000 years ago, but there's no evidence that they distilled alcohol. Instead, they wasted their invention on producing drinkable water.

Most scholars attribute the invention of distilling alcohol to various different North African Arab scientists of the tenth century AD. But these people were chemists. They were interested in the chemistry and not (necessarily) in getting drunk. There's a lot of argument about this and some people think that Abu Nuwas (see Chapter 10) mentions spirits. But nobody can really tell. And certainly the idea didn't take off in either Africa or Europe.

After that there are all sorts of promising leads: things that *sound* like spirits, but may not be. For example, in the twelfth century some English soldiers of Henry II were merrily plundering a monastery in Ireland when they came across some barrels of an unidentified drink that burned their throats and got them very foozled very fast. That *sounds* like spirits, and it may well be. Monasteries were, after all, centers of both science and drinking. But it might just have been strong, spiced ale. We shall never, ever know.

It doesn't help that medieval books on alchemy and medicine tend to be written in code, or just terribly obscure. But you start to get, in the fifteenth century or so, mentions of distilled alcohol being used as a medicine in very small doses. But presumably some invalids found that their medicine tasted good and got them drunk. These people wanted more. But it would still be very expensive.

James IV of Scotland bought several barrels of whisky, or aqua vitae as it was called, from a monastery in 1495. The order seems to have been for the equivalent of several hundred bottles, more than is needed for health purposes. But James IV was a king and could afford it, and the monastery was a specialized institution and probably one of a very, very few places that could make spirits in bulk.

A hundred years later, there was one bar in England—just outside London—that served aqua vitae. It was still a novelty drink that most people would never even have heard of. And then, in the second half of the seventeenth century, western Europe went crazy for spirits. The French suddenly got into brandy, and the Dutch got into *jenever*. The English, meanwhile, were busy having a civil war and then being ruled by Puritans, who weren't much interested in spirits.

Come the Restoration, the English aristocracy stampeded back from France with a newfound taste for all sorts of funny newfound drinks: champagne, vermouth, and brandy. These became the drinks of the nobility. But the English weren't too sure about their new Frenchified aristocracy, and in 1688 things came to a head when England sent their monarch back into French exile, and imported a new Dutch monarchy instead, under the name of William and Mary. And it was William who brought the gin.

Gin

Gin became popular in England for four reasons: monarchy, soldiers, religion and an end to world hunger. If you think about it, these are all good reasons. Some historians would add "hatred of the French," which makes five.

First, monarchy. King William III liked gin because he was Dutch and all Dutch people liked gin.

Second, soldiers. Dutch soldiers liked gin for two reasons. Because they were Dutch and because gin infused Dutch soldiers with a peculiar form of bravery, which to this day we refer to as Dutch courage. Third, during this period European countries were constantly going to war with each other, usually on a Protestant vs. Catholic basis. England and Holland were both Protestant, so English soldiers fought alongside the Dutch, and drank alongside the Dutch, and came home with a hangover and a taste for gin. Gin was thus soldierly and Protestant.

Fourth, an end to world hunger. From time immemorial, and probably before, every country in the world had had a problem with Bad Harvests. In a normal year farmers produced just enough grain to feed everybody. They didn't produce any more than that, because they wouldn't be able to sell it. Every so often, though, you got a year with a Bad Harvest. When this happened there wasn't enough grain to go around, and farmers were not in the slightest bit upset.

A funny aspect of the economics of farming is that a Bad Harvest means less grain; less grain means higher grain prices; these higher prices mean that farmers made just as much money from a Bad Harvest as they did from a good one, and it was less work.

The people who suffered from Bad Harvests were the poor and the needy and the government. The government suffered most of all because they had to put up with the whining of the poor and the needy and their rioting.

William III thought he had this problem solved. Gin is

made out of grain, and the quality of the grain doesn't particularly matter. Once the stuff has been fermented and distilled, you can't taste the difference. Therefore, if he could make gin popular in England he would produce a great big market for excess grain during normal years; and that meant that when a Bad Harvest came round there would be an excess to cover it. It might not be the highest-quality excess, but it would be edible. Thus he could end starvation forever. But to do so he'd have to make gin really, really popular.

To do that, you'd have to make gin more readily available than beer. You'd have to make it completely tax-free and unregulated and let anybody who wants to start distilling distill. Also, you'd have to ban the import of French brandy. But William III was doing that anyway, because like all sensible English monarchs he had already gone to war with France.

And that's how Madam Geneva, the xenophobic daughter of a Dutch mother and an English squaddie, arrived in the terrifying metropolis of London.

London

London in 1700 was the largest city in Europe. This was a problem. English society was a remarkably well-ordered thing provided that people lived together in small units, preferably villages. There was no proper police force, but in a village you don't really need one. Everybody knew everybody. There were very few domestic laws, by our standards, but you didn't really need them. As long as you lived in a village, where everybody has their nose firmly ensconced in everybody else's business, social pressure was enough to keep the norms of society in force. The world could be kept in order with a good bit of gossip and some tutting. Nobody could get above their station, nobody could pretend they were something other than they were, nobody could escape their past.

There was even a system of social security, the parish. Any poor parishioner who had fallen on hard times could throw themselves on the parish, and get a little something. Not a lot. But absolute poverty was, usually, kept at bay.

Then everybody moved to London. They didn't do this all at once, but for our purposes they might as well have done. A rumor went round that the streets of London were paved with gold. There were fortunes to be made for the men, and fortunes to be married for the women. In London anything was possible, anybody could become whatever they wanted to be. London was different.

And London, to be fair, really was different. There were only two other towns in England with a population of over 20,000. London had 600,000. Nobody had seen anything like it before. Aspects of life were entirely new. You could be anonymous. People were surprised that you could walk down a street and not meet *anybody* you knew. This was so astonishing that people wrote newspaper articles about it.

You could dress up. And if you dressed as a gentleman, nobody knew you weren't one. This was astonishing too. It was also fundamentally bamboozling to the whole social order. That chap, who looked like a gentleman, might not be one; and that chap in rags might have been one yesterday—this was the time of the first great stock-market collapse, known as the South Sea Bubble. London was filled with people who claimed to have distinguished war records and would beat you up for not calling them Captain. You could act up and act out and nobody knew who you were so you could get away with it. Anything was possible, including absolute poverty. The thing about the parish system of social security is that it only worked in your native parish. In London, if you were poor, you were on your own.

Not entirely on your own. There were a lot of other poor people. They lived in slums and shanty towns built around Westminster and the East End. The people who lived there were thoroughly, thoroughly miserable. They needed to forget. They needed some kind of drink that was entirely unregulated, that could get you really damned drunk really damned fast, and that was entirely untaxed and therefore very, very cheap. They needed to drink till they passed out on a pauper's bed. They needed the motherly comfort of Madam Geneva; or, as the standard slogan put it, "Drunk for a penny. Dead drunk for tuppence. Clean straw for nothing."

Drinking Gin

Throughout this book, I've been trying to record the where, when, and who of drinking. For all the socio-economic brouhaha outlined above, where did a poor

Londoner actually go to get gin? And when? And from whom? And the answer is absolutely everywhere, and anytime, and anyone.

To set up a gin shop you needed next to nothing. Well, you needed gin. To get that you went to one of the big distillers (called the malt distillers) and bought a gallon or so of raw spirit. You took it home and then you distilled it a *second* time. This is important as it made their gin much more potent than the modern stuff. Scholars argue, but it was about 80 percent ABV, about double anything you'd get today. While doing your secondary distilling you could chuck in some flavorings. Juniper is important (but not indispensable, as we shall see), and you could add anything else that took your fancy. Something to give it a kick. Turpentine was a favorite, as was sulfuric acid. This was not good for you. It doesn't matter. Now you've got a gin shop.

A gin shop was a small room in a poor building. That was it. The *London Magazine* noted that in poor areas "it is sold in some part or other of almost every house, frequently in cellars, and sometimes in the garret." They weren't exaggerating. It's reckoned that in St. Giles (just south of where the British Museum is today) one room in five was a gin shop, packed full of the dirty poor drinking away their sorrows or sleeping away their drinks.

And if you can't be bothered with the stairs to the basement or the garret, you can buy it on the street. Anywhere. From anyone.

No modern rabble can long subsist without their darling cordial, the good preservation of sloth, geneva, that infallible antidote against care and frugal reflection; which, being repeated, removes all pain of sober thought, and in a little time cures the tormenting sense of the most pressing necessities. The traders who send it among the mob on these occasions are commonly the worst of both sexes, but most of them weather-beaten fellows that have misspent their youth. There stands an old sloven, in a wig actually putrefied, squeezed up in a corner, and recommends a dram of it to the goers-by. There another in rags, with several bottles in a basket, stirs about with it where the throng is the thinnest, and tears his throat with crying his commodity; while, further off, you may see the head of a third, who has ventured into the middle of the current, and minds his business as he is fluctuating in the irregular stream [he's talking about a Thames boatman]. Whilst, higher up, an old decrepit woman sits dreaming with it on a bulk, and over against her in a soldier's coat, her termagant daughter sells the sot's-comfort with great dispatch. The intelligible sounds that are heard among them are oaths and vile expressions, with wishes of damnation at every other word, pronounced promiscuously against themselves, or those they speak to, without the least alteration in the meaning.

How much did you drink? Pints of the stuff. Now, you may think that unlikely. I mentioned above that this stuff could get to 80 percent ABV, and a human can't drink pints of that and live. So people didn't. They died. The number of accounts of people dropping down dead in a gin shop is phenomenal and depressing. In 1741 some Londoners met a farm laborer in Newington Green, on the edge of the countryside. For a laugh they persuaded him "in a Frolick, as they call'd it, to drink three or four Pints of Gin giving him a Shilling for each Pint, which he had no sooner done, but he fell down, and died immediately."

That particular example is pleasantly symbolic. Partially because it was a country bumpkin arriving in London and dying immediately of gin. But also because *he wouldn't have known*. The peasantry were used to drinking pints of ale, and they were used to drinking them at any time of day, including breakfast. Why not drink a pint of this new stuff?

To us, the answer is obvious. But we have the benefit of a society that has spent 300 years socializing spirits. A new drug is a dangerous thing, not because the drug is dangerous in and of itself, but because the culture has not yet laid down rules on how to consume it. It is theoretically possible that in some distant future we will have thoroughly socialized crack cocaine. Everybody will know that you only, of course, smoke crack on a Thursday at teatime, and that you only do one very small crystal. Your grandmother will heat the pipe while you make polite conversation with the vicar as he passes round the crumpets. Crack is *always* served with crumpets.

But that's not how it works today. And that's not how gin was consumed then. It didn't have to be pints. The usual quantity was a quartern, or quarter-pint. And you could water it down if you felt like it. Nonetheless, the amounts would make any modern drinker ill.

Drinking was out of control, which was something

that was very frightening to those who were meant to control society—the upper classes. There was a chap called William Bird who had a nice house in Kensington. He also had a maidservant called Jane Andrews. One day in March 1736, William went out and left Jane in charge of the house. Jane, being a responsible girl,

> shut up his doors, and went to Kensington Town to a Gin-shop she usually frequented, and there found a drummer of the guards of her acquaintance, a chimney-sweeper, and a woman traveller. She invited [them] home to her master's house where they drank plentifully from ten in the morning till four in the afternoon, when Jane Andrews proposed to the company . . . that they and she should all go to bed together; and thereupon they shut up the doors and windows, and tho 'twas but about four o'clock in the afternoon, they stript, and all four went into one bed together (as the Maid called it *to ring changes*) and lay there till a mob, hearing of this affair, surrounded the door, and disturbed the happy pairs.

This story is disturbing not just because of what a chimney sweeper would do to your nice clean sheets, but because of the social disorder it represents. Imagine being a rich servant-employing kind of chap and reading about it in the papers. You'd be afraid to ever leave your house again. When a chimney sweeper is ringing changes in *your* bed, that's practically revolution.

The other spine-tingling aspect of the story is that Jane was a woman, as was Madam Geneva. Women loved their gin. It was an entirely unisex drink. Beer had been drunk by the fairer sex, but not in huge quantities. Gin, perhaps because it was metropolitan, perhaps because it was new and fashionable, was the lady's favorite. This bothered men, who wrote innumerable pamphlets about how gin made girls licentious and bawdy (which was a bad thing) and drove them to sex, which drove them to pregnancy, during which the consumption of huge amounts of gin damaged the fetuses (this was actually true). And then, when the deformed baby was born, gin made them bad mothers and bad nursemaids. This last bit was true as well, I'm afraid. There was one nursemaid called Mary Estwick who let the child she was meant to be looking after catch fire while she was passed out drunk. You might think that this counted as negligence, but the coroner ruled that she was a good woman and that it was all "owing to that pernicious Liquor." Anyway, there was another nursemaid who did rather worse when she was putting fuel onto a fire, and mistook the baby for a log with predictable consequences. And there was Judith Defour, who was destined to become the face of gin.

Judith Defour was a poor woman, and she liked her gin. She had a baby girl called Mary who was two years old. The father was long gone and Judith couldn't afford to feed her child, so she sent her to live at the parish workhouse, which gave her a nice new set of clothes. One Sunday morning Judith walked out from the top of Brick Lane across the fields to the workhouse and asked to take Mary out for the day.

They left at about ten in the morning, and, sometime

during the afternoon, Judith met a woman called Sukey and they started drinking gin together. Then at about 7 p.m. they ran out of money. According to Judith it was Sukey who had the bright idea of selling Mary's clothes to pay for more gin. It was January, so it was already dark. They stripped little Mary of her clothes, and they left her in a ditch in the fields, and they set off back into London to get their gin. But Mary was crying, crying in her cold ditch, and Judith couldn't leave her crying. So Judith Defour went back to Mary, took her out of the ditch, and strangled her until she was dead. Then she put her daughter's body back in the ditch and went off to get drunk. In her own words: "And, after that, we went together, and sold the coat and stay for a shilling, and the petticoat and stockings for a groat. We parted the money, and joined for a quartern of gin."

Later that night, Judith Defour told her work colleagues what she had done. She was tried, and hanged.

It's important to note that not all women were murdering their children for gin. According to her mother, Judith Defour "was never in her right mind, but was always roving." It's always hard with the gin craze to tell how much is made-up horror story and how much is real horror story. There were, after all, at least two cases of women who drank gin and spontaneously combusted.* Nonetheless, Judith Defour personified everything that everybody hated about gin and led directly to the Gin Act of 1736.

---

* These were taken quite seriously and were discussed by the Royal Society.

Banning

Gin arrived in England in the 1690s. By the 1720s people had begun to notice that the streets of London were filled with unconscious drunks who had sold their clothes for gin (public nudity was another problem). In 1729 the first Gin Act was passed regulating and taxing gin, which was defined as a strong spirit flavored with juniper. The distillers got around this one by cunningly not adding juniper to their spirits. They just sold pure hooch, and then, just to pile insult upon injury, they called it "parliamentary brandy."

An equally effective act was passed in 1733, but after the affair of Ms. Defour things got a touch more serious. The 1736 act required all gin sellers to get a license, and that license cost £50 a year, which was a huge amount of money by the standards of the time—well north of £10,000 in modern terms. People got around this one by the cunning expedient of not getting a license and selling gin anyway. In fact, only two licenses were ever taken out.

So the government, needing to show they were in charge, offered a bounty to anyone who was prepared to rat on an illegal gin seller. The bounty was substantial and a lot of people became informers. The public got around this one by cunningly banding into mobs and beating informers to death. Meanwhile, to get their gin, they resorted to fake cats.

As the inventor of the fake cat, Dudley Bradstreet, wrote an autobiography, I feel it only fair to tell his story in his words:

The mob being very noisy and clamorous for want of their beloved Liquor, which few or none at last dared to sell, it soon occurred to me to venture upon that trade. I bought the Act, and read it over several times, and found no Authority by it to break open Doors, and that the informer must know the name of the person who rented the house it was sold in. To evade this, I got an acquaintance to take a house in Blue Anchor Alley in St. Luke's Parish, who privately convey'd his bargain to me; I then got it well secured, and . . . purchased in Moorfields the Sign of a Cat, and had it nailed to a Street Window; I then caused a leaden pipe, the small end out about an inch, to be placed under the paw of the cat; the end that was within had a funnel to it.

When my house was ready for business, I enquired what Distiller in London was the most famous for good gin, and was assured by several, that it was Mr. L—dale in Holborn: to him I went and laid out thirteen pounds, which was all the money I had, except two shillings, and told him my scheme, which he approved of. This cargo was sent off to my house, at the back of which there was a way to go in or out. When the liquor was properly disposed, I got a person to inform a few of the mob, that gin would be sold by the Cat at my window next day, provided they put the money in its mouth, from whence there was a hole that conveyed it to me. At night I took possession of my den, and got up early next morning to be ready for custom; it was near three hours before anybody called, which made me almost despair of the project; at last I heard the chink of money, and a comfortable voice say, "Puss, give me two pennyworth of gin." I instantly put my mouth to the tube, and bid them receive it from the pipe under her paw, and then measured and poured it into the funnel, from whence they soon received it. Before night I took six shillings, the next day above thirty shillings, and afterwards three or four pounds a day.

He blew his money on whores and oysters.

Puss-and-mew machines, as they were called, became popular all over London. Crowds of poor people gathered around drinking from a cat. It made the Gin Act look rather silly; it made the government look powerless; and it must have made London look extraordinary.

So the government passed more gin acts. Too many to bore you with here. The important idea that they came up with in the 1740s was not to try and ban gin outright, nor to tax it a lot, but to tax it a little, and then to slowly raise those taxes. It was a nice idea, but for some reason gin consumption started to fall anyway. The glamour was off. The fashion was dying. And then, in the 1750s, something amazing happened: there was a series of Bad Harvests.

The grain shortages that William of Orange had planned for sixty years before finally came to pass, and there was still enough to make bread for everyone. It was a miracle, and, as long as you weren't dead or spontaneously combusted, gin had done its job.

The craze was past. But gin had changed British society irrevocably. It had made the ruling classes very scared of the urban poor. It wasn't just that they didn't like their drinking, it was that they didn't like their lawlessness, their disrespect for the law, and their organization into mobs. Gin created a visible underclass on the pavements of London. And the only sensible thing to do with a visible underclass is to deport it to another continent. And that's how America and Australia were born.

CHAPTER 15

AUSTRALIA

Australia was meant to be a dry colony. Of all the plans in history that didn't quite come off—Napoleon's advance on Moscow, Mao's Great Leap Forward, Hitler's Thousand-Year Reich—this is my favorite.

Lord Sydney, who thought up Australia, had a rather utopian, terribly moral idea of what the place would be. The convicts were not being sent there to suffer, but to reform, and the agency of reform would be hard work and fresh air and nature and vaguely uplifting stuff like that. There would be no alcohol and no money—because without those there would be no crime.

The plan did not get very far. In fact, it got as far as Plymouth. The First Fleet, which set sail in 1787, consisted of three groups. There were the convicts, the marines who were there to guard the convicts, and the privately contracted sailors who were going to steer them there, and then come straight home. The sailors were allowed to take some booze. The marines were told that they couldn't. The marines didn't take this well. In fact, they were "sorely aggrieved" and wrote a memo to their commanding officer to say so. They added that alcohol was "an indispensable requirement for the preservation of our lives, which change of climate and the extreme fatigue . . . may probably endanger."

Lord Sydney was informed of the "discontent in the garrison," and he backed down, but only partially. He allowed the marines (and only the marines) to have alcohol for the first three years of the colony's existence. After that, Australia would be dry at last.

The Australia that might have been was a wonderful place. An early draft of the instructions for the first governor—which form a sort of manifesto for the nation—specifies that he should:

cause the laws against blasphemy, profaneness, adultery, fornication, polygamy, incest, profanation of the Lord's Day, swearing, and drunkenness to be rigorously executed . . .

And, I suppose, it partly worked, or at least I've never heard of an Australian polygamist.

Anyhow, the First Fleet got to Australia and the unloading began. This was more complicated than it sounds. First, the marines got off. Then a few days later the male convicts were landed. A few days after that the female convicts landed. The Fleet's surgeon described the merry event: "The men convicts got to them very soon after they landed, and it is beyond my ability to give a just description of the scene of debauchery and riot that ensued during the night." God showed his opinion by killing seven of the colony's sheep with a lightning bolt, and one pig.

But the real problem was when to unload the booze. Arthur Phillip, the first governor, had seen what had happened to the women, and he didn't want the same fate to befall something that he felt had actual value. So the colony's booze was left waiting in the First Fleet's store ship, the *Fishburn*, until they could construct a secure warehouse in which to store the spirits.* Phillip was perfectly correct to take such care; during his governorship the majority of all crimes in the colony would be either attempts to steal the precious drink, or violence committed under its influence.

Exactly when the first attempts at homebrewing were made is a vexed question, but we can conservatively estimate that it was on day one. It was certainly recorded by 1793. Australia's landscape was (and is) an unfriendly place where all plant and animal life was (and is) designed by a venomous and vengeful God. But to imagine the true horror of New South Wales you have to remember that there was at this time no such thing as refrigeration or air-conditioning. This was Australia without a cold beer. For the early years, everything is down to rum.

The good stuff still had to be imported. In 1792 a ship called the *Royal Admiral* arrived in Sydney Cove loaded with rum and beer. Phillip said that they could sell the beer, but not the rum. So the captain sold the beer legally,

* I've not been able to establish it for certain, but so far as I can tell New South Wales's first building was a secure booze-bunker.

and the rum illegally. The jolly results were recorded by the chaplain.

> Much intoxication was the consequence. Several of the settlers, breaking out from the restraint to which they had been subject, conducted themselves with the greatest impropriety, beating their wives, destroying their stock, trampling on and injuring their crops in the ground, and destroying each other's property.

In 1792, Phillip gave up and went home. He was replaced by Francis Grose,* who had a slightly better answer to the booze question. If you couldn't stop the flow of spirits into the colony, you might as well take control of it. Spirits *were* still illegal, and back in Britain the government still fondly dreamed that New South Wales was a sober hive of morally improving industry. So when, in 1793, another rum ship turned up in the cove, Grose announced that he didn't want to buy the rum, really didn't want to buy it, but felt that he was "forced" to do so in order to keep it from the convicts. Grose then distributed it to his fellow soldiers, who sold it on to the convicts at a markup of around 1,200 percent.

Lieutenant Governor Grose was a soldier, a member of the special battalion that had been formed to guard the new colony: the New South Wales Corps, also known as the 102nd Regiment of Foot, also known as the Botany

---

* The son of Francis Grose, the enormous lexicographer and watercolorist.

Bay Rangers, also known as the Rum Corps, the Rum Puncheon Corps, the Rum Regiment and the Condemned. The Rum Corps were the worst soldiers in the British army. Many of them had quite literally been chucked out of other regiments, and had accepted conscription to Australia as a substitute for court martial, prison or hanging (others chose to be hanged). Australia was not a glamorous destination. There were no glorious wars to be fought, no fortunes to be made, no beautiful generals' daughters to woo. There was very little to drink. This wasn't India or South Africa, or anywhere pleasant. This was an unfarmed, unrefrigerated and unfriendly continent where all of the women were, quite literally, convicted prostitutes. There was no money to be made, because there was, quite literally, no money. That part of Lord Sydney's plan still held.

So, what did the soldiers sell their rum for? The answer is central to understanding how the colony worked. It was a barter economy where work was exchanged for food, for land or for anything else that you happened to have. The majority of the population were convicts whose labor was forced; if you wanted them to do anything more than they already had to do, you had to offer them something. And the only *thing* in this antipodean hellhole that gave *pleasure* was rum. This meant that whoever controlled the rum supply controlled the colony. This was the genius of Lieutenant Governor Grose.

Most historians will tell you that rum was the currency of New South Wales, but it was more than that. It was an instrument of social control. Rum was a paradox: control of its distribution was a form of tyranny, but its consumption created anarchy. For the next twenty years the Rum Corps would control the rum business, which made them rich, but more importantly made them all-powerful. A succession of governors would arrive from London with orders to stop the trade in spirits, but they couldn't because the trade in spirits was the one and only lever of power.

The next governor to arrive was John Hunter in 1795. He had a piece of paper with him ordering the end of the rum trade. The soldiers politely told him what he could do with the piece of paper. A helpful young lieutenant called John Macarthur explained to him that rum was the only thing that made the convicts work, and Hunter felt that there was nothing he could really do. He knew that distributing alcohol to a population composed entirely of criminals might be foolish, but he went along with it. A year into his governorship he noted, rather ruefully, that rum had led to:

> the almost total extinction of every spark of religion; to the encouragement of gambling; the occasion of frequent robberies; and concerned am I to add, to several very recent and shocking murders, and in short, to the abolition of all discipline and every attention to the concerns of government.

But it had its upsides. God, for example, required rum, insofar as the first church in Australia was built with convict labor. The convicts were rewarded with 50 pounds of meat, 3 pounds of tobacco, 5 pounds of tea and 20 gallons of rum. The convicts probably got a warm fuzzy feeling inside with the knowledge that they were doing the Lord's work, but that too may have been down to the rum.

And rum had all sorts of downsides. We don't have many accounts of what a drinking session actually looked like. But gambling seems to have been a staple ingredient. That was certainly the opinion of the colony's only (ungrateful) priest, who said of drunken betting that:

> To such excess was this pursuit carried among the convicts, that some had been known, after losing provisions, money,* and all their spare clothing, to have staked and lost the very clothes on their wretched backs, standing in the midst of their associates as naked, and as indifferent about it, as the unconscious natives of the country.

Importantly, people weren't drunk all the time. Alcohol was limited, because it was only by limiting its supply that the Rum Corps could remain rich and powerful. The commandant of the corps wrote, in a rare fit of honesty, that "the excessive restraints which have been imposed upon the importation of spirituous liquors have very powerfully contributed to heighten the desire of the colonists to possess them, and have absolutely increased the evils which they were intended to diminish."

So the cargo of the *Hope* was an instrument of social chaos and simultaneously of social control. The convicts "hesitated not [so saith the priest] to go any lengths to

---

* By this time, copper coins and Spanish dollars were dribbling into the economy.

procure it, and preferred receiving liquor for labour, to every other article of provisions or clothing that could be offered them."

The Rum Rebellion

The colony needed sorting out. It needed drying out. And it needed somebody who could slap down the troublesome Rum Corps. It needed somebody that nobody would ever disobey, let alone mutiny against. It's therefore somewhat surprising that in 1806 the British government appointed as governor Captain William Bligh; and, yes, that is the same Captain Bligh from the mutiny on the *Bounty*. The government reckoned, I suppose, that that had all happened seventeen years previously, and nobody would ever mutiny against Bligh again.

Bligh was not an easy fellow to get along with. His general view of the world was that everybody else was wrong and that he was right. His view of the New South Wales Corps was that they were, at best, "tremendous buggers, wretches and villains."*

Bligh didn't like this "dangerous militia" at all. He certainly didn't like the way they ogled his daughter, Mary, and

---

* "Bugger," at this time, would almost certainly have meant "homosexual." It's a little odd, as many historians think that the mutiny on the *Bounty* was the direct result of some kind of funny relationship between Bligh and Fletcher Christian. When asked to give a physical description of Christian, Bligh mentioned a tattoo on his bottom. There may be an innocent explanation for this, I just can't think of one offhand.

he was not prepared to compromise in the slightest. He was up against Captain John Macarthur, who was a dishonest, scheming soldier-bootlegger who had made himself the richest man in the colony. Bligh was a straight-up-and-down bastard. Macarthur was a crafty lying bastard.

Bligh confiscated Macarthur's stills. Macarthur was furious and demanded that Bligh return his (utterly illegal) property. Bligh refused and doubled down by summoning Macarthur to court. Macarthur went to court quite happily. He knew that the jury would have to be composed of soldiers and free settlers, all of whom he had in his pocket, and all of whom had already taken a dislike to Bligh. On the day of the trial the jury actually started cheering Macarthur, as did the soldiers who had ostentatiously gathered around the courthouse. Bligh, who had been born furious, became furiouser and furiouser. He sent for the commander of the regiment, Major George Johnston, demanding that he get his men under control. Johnston replied with a note saying that he was sorry, but he had been drunk the night before and crashed his carriage, so there wasn't a thing he could do as he was a little sore.

Bligh stormed back to the Governor's Mansion and began to wonder what his next move should be. Macarthur, on the other hand, already knew what his next move was. It involved rum.

When the soldiers released Macarthur from jail later that day, he had a letter ready, a letter that implored George Johnston to arrest William Bligh and take command of the colony. He was immediately able to get 140 signatures. That evening 300 soldiers gathered at the barracks. They had a drink. Then they advanced on the Governor's Mansion singing songs and playing musical instruments. It was a rather jolly affair. There was almost no resistance. In fact, the only person to stand in their way was Bligh's daughter, Mary, who tried to take on 300 soldiers using only her parasol. Bligh was found hiding under a bed.

On January 26, 1808, twenty years to the day after the landing of the First Fleet, Australia had its only military coup. The day is still celebrated as Australia Day (because of the landing, not the coup), and the whole event is known to history as the Rum Rebellion.

George Johnston was now ruler of Australia. He had been the first soldier to set foot on the continent. He had been there since the beginning. He had even married a convict, a lace-thief named Esther Abrahams, who was now first lady. Effigies of Bligh were burned in the streets, and the soldiers celebrated by roasting sheep, because, this being Australia, everything must end with a barbecue.

And they drank rum.

Macquarie

Discipline, personified by Bligh, had failed, and Australia was now in the hands of the soldiers, in the pockets of the dishonest and in the grip of rum. And this is where the British government had their great stroke of genius. In 1809 they sent out a new governor, a governor perfect for that perfidious continent, a governor who was a soldier, a dipsomaniac and a crook. His name was Lachlan Macquarie, and the Rum Corps never stood a chance.

Macquarie's genius consisted in realizing that everybody was a crook, accepting it, celebrating it and then outcrooking them all. That's how the Australian healthcare system began.

Sydney didn't have a proper hospital. It had a shack. So when Macquarie arrived with strict instructions from Lord Castlereagh, the Secretary of State for the Colonies, to "prohibit the use of spirituous liquors," he threw them away, and made hospitals his first order of business. He decided that he would pay for the plan by selling a monopoly, a monopoly on rum.

Macquarie approached three rich free settlers and made them his offer: the exclusive right to import 60,000 gallons of rum over the next three years in exchange for one shiny new hospital. He even had the plans ready and drawn up. The investors looked at the offer and realized that they would make an absolute killing. The price of a hospital was as nothing compared to the value of the booze concession. The soldiers probably looked on and planned how they would work around this. Nobody looked at the small print.

Macquarie had a clause in the contract saying that the government would retain the right to sell off any spirits that they already owned. It was an innocuous-looking clause, and it wouldn't have meant a thing, were it not that Macquarie had secretly stockpiled 76,000 gallons of rum.

By the time the investors understood, it was too late.

Macquarie got £40,000 worth of hospital in exchange for nothing, indeed for less than nothing, as he continued to tax the rum that they wearily imported, making another £9,000 in cash. Australia's health-care system had begun, and it was built on a con.

The only downside was that the hospital wasn't that good. There was no morgue, which was optimistic, and there were no lavatories, which was unrealistic; and the building, which was immediately christened the Rum Hospital, soon became known as the Sydney Slaughter-house. It is now the New South Wales Parliament. But the building's failings are almost certainly down to Macquarie's one failing: he loved his wife. Macquarie liked to name things, and he named them after Elizabeth Macquarie. To this day you can go shopping in Sydney on Elizabeth Street or sailing in Elizabeth Bay. Or you can visit Mrs. Macquarie's chair near the Botanic Gardens. Elizabeth Macquarie loved architecture. She had a library of books on the subject. She was an enthusiast. Nobody knows for sure who the anonymous architect of the Rum Hospital was, but it was somebody very close to the governor, and pretty much every historian agrees that it was Mrs. Macquarie.

Other Drinks

Australia was built on rum. Rum was a rebellion and rum was a hospital, rum was power and rum was a potable currency. These days we associate Australia with wine and beer, but they are later interlopers and fair-weather friends. The first book published on viticulture in Australia came out in 1803, but it had been translated from the French and the translator had forgotten to reverse the seasons, an omission that resulted in vines being pruned in January. Beer was brewed in small quantities from at least 1790. But it wasn't chilled, and warm beer doesn't really hit the antipodean spot. Now, rum is nearly forgotten in the country she created, which is filled with grapes and Foster's. But we should still remember the (alleged) song of the earliest felonious frontiersmen:

> Cut yer name across me backbone
> Stretch me skin across yer drum
> Iron me up on Pinchgut Island
> From now to Kingdom Come.
> I'll eat yer Norfolk Dumpling
> Like a juicy Spanish plum,
> Even dance the Newgate Hornpipe
> If ye'll only gimme Rum!

CHAPTER 16

THE WILD WEST SALOON

If you meet, you drink; if you part, you drink; if
you make acquaintance, you drink; if you close a
bargain, you drink; they quarrel in their drink, and
they make it up with a drink.

Frederick Marryat, *A Diary in America* (1839)

In 1797 the largest distillery in America produced 11,000 gallons of whiskey a year. It was owned by the great distiller of
early America, a man called George Washington.

Washington's life story is rather extraordinary. Before
becoming a whiskey magnate he had, in fact, had something of a career in politics and even the military. It need
not detain us for long. Essentially, in politics Washington had stood for office and lost. He had then stood for
office and handed out free booze to the voters. This time
he won. His election expenses for the House of Burgesses
of 1758 were as follows:

Dinner for your Friends £3 os od
13 gallons of Wine at 10/ £6 15s od
3 pts of brandy at 1/3 4s 4d
13 gallons of Beer at 1/3 16s 3d
8 qts Cyder Royal at 1/6 12s od
30 gallons of strong beer at 8d £1 os od
1 hhd and 1 barrell of Punch, consisting of 26 gals.
Best Barbados rum at 5/ £6 10s od
12 lbs S. Refd. Sugar at 1/6 18s 9d
10 Bowls of Punch at 2/6 each £1 5s od
9 half pints of rum at 7d each £0 5s 7d
1 pint of wine £0 1s 6d

There were only 600 eligible voters.*

As for his career in the military, it is even less interesting. Essentially, he had the bright idea of doubling his men's rum rations, thus causing a strange phenomenon known as the USA. After that he fought another brief war in order to tax whiskey. And then, at last, he settled down to the serious business of distillation. He produced quite a variety: quadruple distilled whiskey, rye whiskey, cinnamon-flavored whiskey, and brandies made from apple, persimmon and peach. It was a good business to get into because, in this strange new invention called America, spirits were all the rage.

Between 1790 and 1830 spirits consumption in the USA nearly doubled from 5 to 9½ gallons per person per

* Oh, all right. Per voter, that's approximately a pint of beer, a glass of wine and one pint of rum.

183

year. And this taste for spirits was, largely, the result of the great push westward.

When the colonies in North America started they had been simple offshoots of European drinking culture, and therefore revolved around beer. The Pilgrim Fathers weren't meant to land at Plymouth Rock, but the *Mayflower* had run out of beer. So they had to stop there.

Breweries had been built because, although the water in this virgin continent was actually all right to drink, the Pilgrims, being European, were still sniffy about drinking water and still obeyed the (oft-adapted) rule of Aelfric mentioned in Chapter 9: "Beer if I have it, water if I have no beer." Or as a Puritan settler called William Wood put it: American water "was of a fatter substance, and of a more jetty colour; it is thought there can be no better water in the world . . . Yet I do not prefer it before a good beer."

But there is one problem with beer and that problem is transport. A barrel of beer is a heavy thing and, compared to a barrel of spirits, it doesn't contain very much alcohol. If you are a settler heading west into the great unknown, with limited space and weight in your wagon train, a barrel of whiskey will get you a lot drunker a lot farther. The second you are out of the reach of civilization and the brewery (the two things being identical), you want to have that barrel of spirits, and what better place to buy it from than Mount Vernon? It was, after all, named after the British Admiral Edward Vernon, who wore a grogram coat and was nicknamed Old Grog. Vernon watered down his sailors' rum rations, thus also giving his name to the word *grog*.

Whenever an American went out into the wilds they

took with them a barrel of whiskey (or peach brandy if they were feeling *fabulous*), and so the farther you got from New York, Philadelphia, Boston and the beer-swilling world of the eastern seaboard, the more you found that beer had been replaced by spirits. And the replacement was that simple. New Yorkers, like their British counterparts, still drank beer for breakfast. And so a Kentucky breakfast was defined (in 1822) as "three cocktails and a chaw of terbacker."

A cocktail here is in essence exactly what it sounds like: a "*Cock tail*, then, is a stimulating liquor, composed of spirits of any kind, sugar, water, and bitters" (1806). Whiskey for breakfast could be considered a challenge even then, so by mixing in a little fruit juice, or whatever came to hand, you could take in all the health-giving benefits of an alcoholic breakfast (which were still believed in) and not vomit.

So, a curious passenger pigeon in the first half of the nineteenth century would have seen thousands of people heading slowly westward. Where were they going and why? The cautious ones would have been heading to just beyond the limits of currently farmed land where they would build themselves a little house and stake a claim. The more ambitious ones were going to the Frontier, to the place where the states of America became undefined wilderness, to what we call the Wild West. Why? Because it was rich.

Hollywood likes to portray the Wild West as a world of relative paupers, a land of poor-but-dishonest men, who occasionally have to endure a moneyed interloper from the East Coast. The reverse is true. People didn't go west to become poor; that would be silly. They went west because wages out there were roughly double what they were on the East Coast. There would be booms—mining booms, fur booms, cattle booms—and there wouldn't be nearly enough labor to supply the market. So wages shot up, while the overpopulated East Coast went hungry.

The downside was that infrastructure didn't follow fast enough. There were no roads or railways, no courthouses or sheriffs, and there were no bars. (There were also very few women, but we shall come to that.) The result was a largish population of rich men with a lot of money and nothing to spend it on (and nobody to stop them being robbed). So wherever the workers went, the ambitious barman followed close behind.

The first saloon that was called a saloon was Brown's Hole in the town of Brown in Utah, and that's the word I shall be using for the rest of the chapter. The idea was, presumably, to sound faintly upmarket and French-ified, something that early Frontier saloons definitely weren't. They would start out as tents. Anybody who was interested in making money might hear about a new mining town, but decide that mining wasn't for them. So they would grab a barrel and a tent and show up. That was it. There was sometimes a wooden board put atop two barrels to serve as a bar, but you weren't getting much more French than that. Here's a description of a Kansas tent saloon:

> It consisted of crotched stakes . . . which supported a ridgepole, across which some old sailcloth was drawn . . .

forming a cabin some six by eight feet, and perhaps from three to five and a half feet high—large enough to contain two whiskey barrels, two decanters, several glasses, three or four cans of pickled oysters and two or three boxes of sardines but nothing of the bread kind whatever. The hotelkeeper probably understood his business better than we did, and had declined to dissipate his evidently modest capital by investing any part of it in articles not of prime necessity.

A standard example of a tent saloonkeeper is Roy Bean, a chap we shall be returning to several times in this chapter. Bean was a crook who, at the time, was beating up his wife in the Texas town of Beanville (no relation). In 1881 he heard that the construction of a new railway had resulted in several workers' camps near the Pecos River. So he sold everything he owned and bought ten 55-gallon barrels of whiskey and a tent. Then he set off and found a camp of 8,000 thirsty men. He pitched his tent and started his new career.

There was, though, a problem. The whole point of the Wild West was that there was next to no legal infrastructure. The nearest courtroom was 200 miles away in Fort Stockton. Those 8,000 railway workers had neither booze nor law. Who was to protect the locals from a ne'er-do-well such as Bean? Luckily a passing Texas Ranger saw the problem. He paid a visit to Roy Bean's saloon and asked him, point blank, if he'd like to be justice of the peace.

Bean said yes.

Becoming justice of the peace was a real move up for a habitual criminal like Bean. It was also great for everybody else in the area as they now had recourse to the law. Everybody was happy. Bean was so happy that he went and shot up the saloon of his main competitor, who was Jewish, which seems to have made this all right, though the question of what was right and wrong was now entirely in the hands of Judge Roy Bean.

Let us leave Judge Bean there and not return to him until we have our next racially aggravated homicide, which won't be for several pages. He has, though, illustrated the general scheme of things. Some sort of business starts (in this case a railway), the business brings employment, employment brings money, money brings saloons, and saloons eventually bring (or in this case become) law courts. But for the moment we're still in a tent.

Often the barman of a tent (if you can dignify him with that appellation) would simply sell his stock and go home. If he wanted to remain, he had two options. First, he could send for more booze. This would involve a transfer of money, some sort of contractual arrangement that he would find it very hard to enforce. Alternatively, he could fake his booze.

There's a book from 1853 called *The Manufacture of Liquors, Wines, and Cordials, without the Aid of Distillation*. It's not as bad as it sounds. Distillation is, surprisingly, still involved. The general argument of the book is that rather than buying whiskey or brandy, the sensible, thrifty saloonkeeper should buy pure alcohol and flavor it, and then claim that it's whiskey or brandy or whatever. The author justifies this by saying that this is what European distillers do anyway, and that the Americans have been Lagging Behind. Also:

> the following directions will insure a saving of from forty to two hundred and fifty per cent per gallon; and the most critical examination will scarcely detect the imitation from the genuine, a chemical test alone being able to indicate the difference of the one from the other.

I'm not sure that's entirely true, but I would suspect that you don't have to be a whiskey buff to see through the recipe for old rye:

> Neutral spirit, four gallons; alcoholic solution of starch, one gallon; decoction of tea, one pint; infusion of almonds, one pint; color with one ounce of the tincture of cochineal, and of burnt sugar, four ounces; flavor with oil of wintergreen, three drops, dissolved in one ounce of alcohol.

"Scotch whiskey," by this book, contained "creasote, five drops." Jamaica rum contains sulfuric acid; only half an ounce of the stuff, but it would probably still show up in the chemical test. These delicate and subtle beverages were given appropriately delicate and subtle names like *coffin-varnish*, *tarantula juice*, *tangle-foot* and *sheep dip*.

Generally speaking, this sort of rotgut declined with the advent of the proper saloon, where "proper" means merely "a permanent structure." Once you have a few permanent structures, you have competition and that makes for a better product.

Both the competition and the permanent structures would arrive pretty quickly. When a railway camp was set up at Minot, North Dakota, the new town (if you can call it that) had twelve saloons by the time it was five weeks old. The next move up from a tent would be the dugout, which was a sort of lean-to excavated into a hillside with water dripping from the ceiling. Such an edifice cost one saloonkeeper the grand total of $1.65, in an age when a farm laborer would be earning about 60 cents a day. When he needed to expand again, it cost $500 to build a false-front saloon. The final part of the saloon was the most expensive. Five years later the bar arrived, carved in hard-wood and transported by mule. It cost, including transport, $1,500.

So what did the finished product look like and what was it like to drink in? Hollywood usually has one huge saloon in the center of town. This is a dramatic require-ment as it forces the hero to confront the villain. But, as we've seen, there were usually loads of saloons in town, and in reality hero and villain would have been able to have a quiet drink without ever bumping into each other. A saloon was usually quite a narrow building, preferably on a corner as that upped the value of the signage.

The first and most obvious thing you'd notice would be the false front. This was a two-story façade that was nailed onto the front of a one-story building. Nobody knows why saloons were built like this. It didn't fool any-one. It physically couldn't have, unless you approached it in a straight line perpendicular to the front door, which was impossible if there were buildings on both sides of the street. The façade had work put into it. There were fake windows on the upper story, and sometimes there was even guttering for a nonexistent roof. The false front was a universal, transparent lie that everybody in America for some reason went along with.*

Outside, there would be the hitching post for your horse; around this would be a huge and inevitable pile of horse manure. There was no sanitation on the Frontier, and ladies wore unfortunately long dresses. Men were (as ever) better off, but their spurs couldn't have been that shiny.

You mount the boardwalk and the famous swinging batwing doors are not there to greet you. Batwing doors are a myth, or almost entirely so. There may have been some in the very, very far southwest of the United States, but they were thoroughly atypical. This is obvious when you think about it. They would have been utterly pointless, providing neither privacy nor protection from the cold. They look fantastic on screen, but in reality the doors were full length or very nearly so. They were, though, double hinged and weighted, so you could have something like that dramatic entrance, so long as you don't let them swing back in your face.

In the movies you are now facing the bar. That's wrong too. You're in a long narrow room, and the bar is down one side, almost always to your left. The bar is, really, a

* There's a moral in there somewhere, but I've no idea what it is.

thing of beauty. It's carved, it's hardwood, often mahogany or walnut, and it has been polished to within an inch of its life. Remember that, as we've seen, it probably cost a lot more than the building that houses it. Above the bar is the mirror. This too is kept scrupulously clean as it's also worth a lot of money. It's as long as the bar itself, and is the other great status symbol of the saloonkeeper. Everything else may be cheap, but that's partly because these two things consumed so much of the capital.

The mirror does actually serve a purpose, perhaps two. It allows those sitting at the bar to keep an eye on anybody approaching them from behind. And it allows them to ogle the naked lady. She hangs upon the opposite wall—a voluptuous pseudoclassical nude. She's not exactly pornographic, but she's not exactly prim. Discretions of posture and lace hide the really private parts, but she is nonetheless there to titillate the lonely cowpoke, who probably hasn't seen a woman in weeks.

Along the bottom of the bar, above the sawdust-covered floor, runs the brass rail. The purpose of this is obscure. But people didn't feel that they were in a saloon until they had one boot on the rail. Strangely, when Prohibition came in in 1920 it was for the brass rail that people hankered, and for which nostalgia ran to its most lachrymose extremities. It's strange, because it was probably covered in saliva. At intervals beneath the rail were the spittoons, ideally at a ratio of one to every four customers. It may look as though everybody in here is suffering from toothache, but they are all, in fact, chewing tobacco.

So you put your boot (smeared with horseshit) on the

brass rail (smeared with saliva) and the barman approaches and asks you, "What's your pleasure?"

You have a nice little think about this. You notice that beneath the mirror there are some bottles of wine and champagne and funny things like crème de menthe. Then you notice that they are covered in dust. They are only there for show. Nobody ever orders them, and if somebody, especially a stranger, ever did, they would be in a lot of trouble with the other customers. The only two drinks you can respectably buy are whiskey and beer. And, frankly, beer is pretty questionable. So you order a whiskey for yourself and one for the guy standing next to you. This is a rule. It doesn't matter that you've never met the fellow before. You must always buy one extra drink on the first go. You'll make it up later when another newcomer buys one for you. But the only thing worse than not buying a drink is not accepting one, which will get you beaten up or worse.

We now come to the most complicated and obscure aspect of saloon etiquette, which, weirdly enough, Hollywood always gets right. When our taciturn hero walks into a saloon, *he never asks how much the drinks cost*. He simply throws some coins on the bar, *and he never gets any change*. This is, historically, absolutely accurate.

There are two kinds of saloon: a one-bit saloon and a two-bit saloon. A two-bit saloon is a very grand affair, it will have a floor show and a chandelier and maybe even a real second story. In a two-bit saloon all of the drinks cost two bits. In a one-bit saloon, all of the drinks (both whiskey *and* beer) cost one bit. A cigar also costs one bit. This is useful, as you never need to ask the price. Often it is simply announced on a sign outside, but you almost certainly would have known.

A bit was one-eighth of a dollar, or 12½ cents. This is awkward as there is no such thing as a half-cent. For a long time, in the Southern states the Spanish dollar was an accepted form of currency. The Spanish dollar could be divided into eight. In fact, it was quite often physically cut into eight parts (or bits) which is why piratical parrots are always banging on about *pieces of eight*. For some reason, this was carried over into American dollars, with the curious consequence that there was no way of finding the exact change for a single drink. Instead, if you were buying only one in a one-bit place, you would hand over a quarter (two bits) and get 10 cents in change. This means that you've spent 15 cents (a "long bit") on your first drink. But when you come to your second drink, you'll be allowed to buy it with a dime (or "short bit"). This was spectacularly silly, sillier even than the false fronts, but it was how things worked.

So, you take the bottle of phlegm-cutter and you pour yourself a drink. Do not pour too little, you will be seen as effeminate, and perhaps forced to drink more and at gunpoint. Do not, though, fill it to the brim. This is seen as grasping and greedy, and the barman will ask you if you're planning to take a bath in it. It's an odd thing that where there are loose laws, there are strict manners.

You raise the glass of stagger-juice to your lips, and you down it in one. This will win you the approbation and respect of the other customers. You've probably also made

yourself ill, but that's a small price to pay. You could follow the path of the man who went into a two-bit saloon
and paid a bit. When this was pointed out to him he said,
"Two-bit house, eh? Well, I thought so when I first came
in, but after I had tasted your whiskey I concluded I was
in a bit house." Daring words, but not as daring as the
man who said he could drink a quart of Cincinnati whiskey. He managed the feat and the silver mounting on his
coffin cost $13.75.

So who is in here? Men. Usually white men. A black
man might be tolerated. Native Americans are banned
by law. But the one group that really, really isn't welcome are the Chinese. It's an odd and inexplicable thing.
The Wild West was full of Chinese immigrants who had
come to work on the railways and everybody hated them.
There doesn't seem to have been any reason for this, but
that only made people hate them more. To return, reluc-
tantly, to Judge Roy Bean in his Texas saloon, he once had
the case brought before him of a man accused of murdering a Chinese chap. Bean consulted his law book and
announced that the law stated clearly that it was illegal to
kill another human, but "he'd be damned if he could find
any law against killing a Chinaman."

Who are the men? That is something of a mystery. It
is terribly bad manners to ask a man either his surname
or his business. You can chat, but it has to be on neutral
topics. It may be simpler to go to the very back of the
room where there is a card game going on. This probably
isn't poker but faro, a much simpler game of pretty much
pure chance. Poker was sometimes played, but as faro has

simple rules, moves faster and allows for any number of players, it usually won out. It's very easy to cheat at faro, and that was a problem, because everybody had a gun.

All of this leads to the delicate question I've been skirting around: what, really, are your chances of being shot? And the answer is nice and clear: nobody really knows. It certainly wasn't as bad as the standard Hollywood scene with a couple of murders a night while the pianist keeps on playing (pianos by the way were big and heavy and hard to transport and therefore limited to the two-bit saloons; the automatic pianolas don't come in until the 1880s). But that observation is unfair on Hollywood. After all, royal families aren't usually as violent as Shakespeare makes them out to be. If the real world were as murderous as drama, there'd be nobody left.

The problem is that the Wild West, by definition, doesn't have an efficient bureaucracy. The Wild West is what happens between two events: the discovery of a source of income, and the arrival of law, order and coroners' reports.

There are, of course, anecdotes. People *were* killed in saloons. Wild Bill Hickok, Jack McCall, Bob Ford, John Wesley Hardin and countless others were gunned down. But then again, there were a lot of saloons and a lot of people. Nobody wrote stories about the jolly evening when a few drinks were consumed and nothing happened. People wanted to write about murder, because murder is fun, and because people wanted to read about murder. And there's the problem. The Wild West was romanticized while it still existed. Judge Roy Bean, in his own lifetime, became a tourist attraction. This wife-beating, murdering, sinophobic blackguard died rich on the proceeds of hundreds of wide-eyed tourists coming to his saloon and being horribly overcharged for rotgut, just so they could say that they had met the famous "Law West of the Pecos." Gunslingers became celebrities. Buffalo Bill, Annie Oakley and Sitting Bull all visited England, where they were introduced to Queen Victoria.

Saloon customers certainly did carry guns. That was perfectly normal, and would probably be a little bit intimidating to anybody who wasn't used to it. They also drew them and sometimes fired them, but they didn't necessarily mean any harm by that. Horace Greeley, who was one of the calmest historians of the Western saloon, observed of its customers that they had a "careless way, when drunk, of firing revolvers, sometimes at each other, and other times quite miscellaneously."

There's probably more truth to this than might meet the casual eye. Take this description of a cowtown saloon where people, just for fun, would shoot the lights:

> The "Klondyke" . . . was the village hot spot and had larger mirrors and bigger hanging kerosene lamps to amuse the cowhands when they got frisky enough to use their guns playfully. The man who owned the Klondyke bought his hanging lamps in large quantities and bought lamp chimneys by the barrel.

Guns were everywhere in the Wild West in a way that would be mind-boggling to us, but conversely if you somehow brought an 1860s cowpoke to a London pub in 2017, his mind would be just as boggled by our casual use of smartphones. Guns were undoubtedly used for murder when murder was called for; but they could just as easily be used to shoot lamps or anything that anybody chose as a target. This frightened and excited the tourists, which is probably why people liked to pull guns on tourists and make them drink or dance or whatever it happened to be. Guns did, though, mean that when a fight broke out it was final. This probably made for fewer fights. One cow-hand put it beautifully:

> I never got into a fight when I was drinking, only when I was sober and knew what I was doing. Because I was always so happy when I was drinking. I loved everybody and everybody seemed to love me.

And that leads us from death to sex.

Respectable women never went into a saloon. There are occasional tales of a female barkeep like Rowdy Kate Lowe who was reputed to have shot five men dead (including two husbands), but they were curiosities. There are, though, saloon girls. These are somewhere in between respectable and rentable. Exactly where is uncertain. They will talk to you. They will hold your hand and listen to your problems and provide all those female comfortable words that the lonely trapper wants. So long as you buy them drinks. The drinks aren't real drinks—they look like whiskey but they're cold tea—and the verbal comfort that they provide is probably not meant. But importantly they're not prostitutes. Or not usually (such things were very hard to quantify even at the time, let alone a century and a half later).

Women were a rare commodity out west. They were valuable, very valuable, and they knew it. Why be a whore when you could make $10 a week chatting? A cynic would say that a lonely man wants sex; a romantic would say that he'd prefer an obviously fraudulent simulacrum of female sympathy just so long as he can believe in it for the next ten minutes, and not taste the cold tea. This is one of the few situations known to science where the romantic is right. If I were a theorizing kind of chap, I would draw a parallel: there were pretend two-story buildings, there was pretend whiskey, and there was pretend affection. Either way, there may be a cathouse out back.

They were a sentimental bunch, the frontiersmen. In the absence of anything else, the evening would end with a sing-along, and the favorite subject for the songs was Mother. Mothers, like explosions and pointillist paintings, seem fantastic from a distance, and these were distant men. A fixture of such sing-alongs was the cowboy's favorite "A Boy's Best Friend Is His Mother."

> Then cherish her with care
> And smooth her silvery hair;
> When gone you will never get another;
> And wherever we may turn
> This lesson we may learn—
> A boy's best friend is his mother.

Or you could go for the less sentimental song that began, "If the ocean was whiskey and I was a duck."

There were no real limits on how long this could all go on for, or how drunk you might get. The horses were still sober and could probably take you home. Indeed, if you forgot your horse or were temporarily unable to mount, somebody might just untie it and let it wander home. Or you could just keep drinking. There was nothing to stop you, and sometimes nothing did. Let us finish up with a rare woman's account of a saloon drunk. Specifically, a California miners' saloon at Christmas 1851:

> The saturnalia commenced on Christmas evening, at the Humboldt [saloon] . . . All day long patient mules could be seen descending the hill, bending beneath casks of brandy and baskets of champagne . . . At nine o'clock in the evening they had an oyster-and-champagne supper . . . which was very gay with toasts, songs, speeches, etc. I believe that the company danced all night. At any rate, they were dancing when I went to sleep, and they were dancing when I woke the next morning. The revel was kept up in this mad way for three days, growing wilder every hour. Some never slept at all during that time. On the fourth day they got past dancing and, lying in drunken heaps about the barroom, commenced a most unearthly howling. Some barked like dogs, some roared like bulls and others hissed like serpents and geese. Many were too far gone to imitate anything but their own animalized selves.

CHAPTER 17

RUSSIA

In 1914, Tsar Nicholas II outlawed the sale of vodka in all Russia. In 1918, Tsar Nicholas II and all of his family were executed in a basement in Yekaterinburg. These two facts are not unrelated.

It's quite possible to follow Nicholas's reasoning. There were two obvious sides to the argument. On the one hand, the First World War was kicking off and Russian soldiers had been losing wars rather regularly of late, largely because they were drunk to the gills. On the other hand, one-quarter of all the state's revenue came from taxes on alcohol, and it's generally not a good idea to suddenly cut off your main income stream as you enter a war.

Historians have an awful lot of fun debating to what extent vodka caused the Russian Revolution. Did the loss of tax destroy the state? Or did the ban exacerbate social tensions? Russian laws then, as now, only really applied to the common folk freezing in their cottages. They were not very happy to know that the rich man in his dacha was still knocking back the "little water" that they loved.

You could also still buy vodka in expensive restaurants; it's just that the poor people couldn't afford that.

There's also the theory that 1914–17 are the only three years in Russian history when the population has been sober enough to notice exactly what their government were doing to them. And when you're doing that to your population, they need lubrication. That was, incidentally, Lenin's opinion. He believed religion was the opium of the masses and alcohol was the alcohol of the masses, which is why he didn't drink much himself and kept the ban on vodka in place. It was only repealed by Stalin in 1925.

If you live in Russia today there's a 23.4 percent chance that your death will be related to alcohol. For tsars the risk was much higher.

At the other end of Russian history, in 987 AD, Vladimir the Great, who was ruler of the infant kingdom, invited envoys of the great religions so that he could pick one for his people. The Jews he dismissed when he found that they had no homeland. The Muslims interested him as they described the carnal pleasures of paradise (Vladimir was "fond of women and indulgence"). But when they told him that their religion forbade alcohol he behaved like a sensible tsar.

> "Drinking," said he, "is the joy of the Russes. We cannot exist without that pleasure."

And so Russia became Christian.
That story is rather more believable than it may sound.

Inviting religious ambassadors and then picking a faith for your whole people was actually reasonably common at the time. That account was written up only about a century later in the *Primary Chronicle*, which is the most authoritative source on early Russian history.*

And at the near end of Russian history, Mikhail Gorbachev launched a temperance campaign in 1985. *Perestroika* was getting going and he went on a televized walkabout and actually talked to real members of the public. One of them complained that essentials like beer were too expensive. Gorbachev replied that alcohol was not a *necessity* of life. Six years later Russian communism came to an end.

The Russians are fond of a drink. They are also fond of making others drink. This is a tendency that goes back a long way. As far back as the 1550s the Holy Roman Empire's ambassador to Russia noted that:

> The Muscovites are indeed masters at talking to others and persuading them to drink. If all else fails one other stands up and proposes the health of the Grand-duke, upon which all present must not fail to drink and drain the cup ... The man proposing the toast stands in the middle of the room, his head bared, states what he desires for the Grand-duke or other lord—happiness, victory, health—and wishes that as much blood may remain in the veins of his enemies as drink in his cup. When he has emptied it he reverses the cup upon his head and wishes the lord good health.

* On account of there not being any others.

This custom gives Russians the unusual ability to enforce drunkenness. Pretty much everywhere else in this book getting sloshed has been optional or forbidden or frowned upon or confined to particular times and places that can be avoided. It's true that many cultures have toasts that all must join, but these tend to involve a drink or two at the beginning of the evening (or the end of mass). A symposium or saloon required drinking once you were there, but you didn't have to go. It is true of course that there has always been social pressure to drink and I would hate to be the Viking who asked for orange juice, but in Russia the enforcement of heavy drinking is part of business, diplomacy and politics.

The name Stalin always comes up in discussions of Russia, which is funny, really, as he wasn't Russian and Stalin wasn't his name.* That Stalin ruled with terror is reasonably well known, and the terror, of course, went all the way up to the top of government. But at the very, very top, at the level of Lavrentiy Beria, who was head of the secret police, and Khrushchev, Stalin ruled with terror and drunkenness.

The method was simple. Stalin would call up his politburo and invite them round for supper. They weren't really allowed to refuse. At supper Stalin made them drink, and drink, and drink; and again, they weren't really allowed to refuse. Khrushchev remembered that:

* He was Georgian and his real name was Iosif Vissarionovich Dzhugashvili. "Stalin" was his revolutionary *nom de guerre*. It means "Steel Man."

Almost every evening the phone rang: "C'mon over, we'll have dinner." Those were dreadful dinners. We would get home toward dawn, and yet we had to go to work . . . Things went badly for people who dozed off at Stalin's table.

Stalin was merely doing to his own cabinet what the Soviets delighted in doing to everybody. The Molotov–Ribbentrop pact of 1939 was celebrated by a dinner that included twenty-two toasts before any food arrived. But Stalin's private dinners had a more nightmarish quality to them. Stalin would laugh till he cried as Beria did an impersonation of the dying screams of Grigory Zinoviev, whose death Stalin had ordered. The dictator would tap out his pipe on Khrushchev's bald head before ordering him to do a Cossack dance. The deputy defense commissar was always getting pushed into a pond.

Stalin himself didn't drink much. At least, he drank a lot less than his guests, and there was a rumor that the vodka he was putting away was in fact water. This was a trick that Beria actually attempted, but he was caught. In the end he was philosophical about it and said, "We've got to get drunk, the sooner the better. The sooner we're drunk, the sooner the party will be over. No matter what, he's not going to let us leave sober."

The point of it all was that the politburo were humiliated, that they were set against each other and that their tongues were loosened. It was very hard to plot against Stalin anyway, but much harder when you had to get drop-dead drunk in front of him every night.

This was nothing new. The terrifying Russian dictator forcing vodka down your throat has a long and occasionally amusing history. The main difference between Stalin and Peter the Great (1672–1725) was that Peter certainly drank as much as he forced on others.

The stories of Peter's drinking vary, and are pretty hard to believe. One account says that he would drink a pint of vodka and a bottle of sherry over breakfast, then eight more bottles, then go out for the day. Another has the same figures but with brandy replacing the vodka. This may just have been possible. Peter was a very burly 6 foot 7, which might have allowed for more than the normal human capacity to hold his liquor (and might also explain his obsession with dwarves).

If Stalin had effectively turned the Russian government into a drinking society, Peter officially turned the Russian government into a drinking society. First he created the Jolly Company, which was a sort of drunken parody of the royal court. To be a member you had to drink to keep up with Peter, which was not a simple matter. He had a clubhouse of sorts that could hold 1,500 people and his pet monkey, and every feast would start with toast after toast of vodka to make sure that everybody was thoroughly spifflicated before the food arrived.

The Jolly Company then morphed into the All-Joking, All-Drunken Synod of Fools and Jesters, which was a parody of the Russian church. But these revelers were the government, as well as being the government's pissed parody. The head of Peter's secret police Konstantin Romodanovsky was a member. Like Beria, he was a boozer and an enforcer of boozing. Romodanovsky had a tame bear who would offer guests a glass of peppered vodka, and was trained to attack them if they refused.

Peter himself had a particular punishment for those caught not drinking: the Great Eagle. This was a giant goblet that held one and a half liters of wine. Those caught abstaining were forced to down it at one go. This applied to everybody, and not just members of the All-Joking Synod. Peter knew the value of drunkenness, the power that came with its enforcement and the power that came with reducing the other fellow to a vomiting wreck. The Danish ambassador once found himself on a ship with Peter the Great and was very quickly unable to drink any more. So he actually tried to escape by climbing the mast and hiding among the sails. But Peter found out and climbed after him with wine bottles in his pocket and, in his mouth, the Great Eagle. The ambassador was forced to drink.

Peter was certainly a great man, and he passed many important reforms, especially against beards, but he was not necessarily a nice man. The Prussian ambassador said that he saw with his own eyes Peter ordering twenty prisoners to be brought to him and twenty drinks. He then drank all the drinks and marked each empty glass by drawing his sword and cheerily cutting off a prisoner's head. He then asked the ambassador if he wanted to have a go.

Stalin was also a great fan of Ivan the Terrible (1530–84) who had pioneered the use of drunkenness as a form of close-range political control. He made his subordinates drink:

If they did not drink themselves into a stupor, or rather a frenzy, then [Ivan's friends] added a second and a third beaker; and those who had no wish to drink or to commit such transgressions they adjured with great rebuke, while they shouted at the tsar: "Behold, this one here, and this one (naming him) does not wish to be joyful at your feast, as though he condemns and mocks you and us as drunkards, hypocritically pretending to be righteous!"

Ivan would be even less subtle about his motivations. He would often bring scribes to his feasts who would note down what everybody said while drunk. These jottings would then be read out to them the next morning, and appropriate punishments handed out. The punishments were imaginative to say the least. Ivan had a roguish way about him of raping and killing (and occasionally releasing hungry bears on to unsuspecting monks, which does sound rather fun). But perhaps his cruelest action was to send more drink to the houses of those who had just left his parties. This would be delivered by soldiers who would stay to make sure that it was all downed on the spot.

Now, all of these could just be amusing stories about the foibles of vodka-sodden autocrats, and there would be nothing strange in that. North Korea's Kim Jong-il is reported to have spent $1 million a year on Hennessy, and even Queen Victoria liked a glass of whisky and claret.* But in Russia it's important, not just because of the

* Not quite as bad as it sounds, I discovered.

pattern and continuity over 500 years, but because what Russian rulers do to their cabinet, they also do to their people. It's all Ivan's fault.

In 1552 Ivan the Terrible besieged and conquered the Tatar city of Kazan. While merrily slaughtering the inhabitants he paused long enough to be impressed by the state-run taverns, or *kabaks* as they were called. The Tatars didn't just tax alcohol, they took all the profit. Ivan hurried back to Moscow and built St. Basil's Cathedral to celebrate. He also nationalized all Russia's bars.

Thus was created a curious system of state-run drinking. The *kabaks* were run by what were effectively civil servants. There was none of the "jolly local tavern keeper heart-of-the-community" figure. The tavern keeper was a government employee tasked with getting as much money out of any town or village as he possibly could. Any change in the law that he needed to help him push vodka on civilians would be enacted. Any do-gooder promoting temperance or a quiet night in would be arrested. An English traveler described how Ivan's new system worked:

> In every great town of his realm he hath a *kabak* or drinking house, where is sold aqua vitae (which they call Russ wine), mead, beer, &c. Out of these he receiveth rent that amounteth to a great sum of money. Some yield 800, some 900, some 1,000, some 2,000 or 3,000 roubles a year. Wherein, besides the base and dishonourable means to increase his treasury, many foul faults are committed. The poor labouring man and artificer, many

times spendeth all from his wife and children. Some use to lay in twenty, thirty, forty roubles or more into the *kabak*, and vow themselves to the pot till all that be spent. And this (as he will say) for the honour of hospodar or the emperor. You shall have many there that have drunk all away to the very skin, and so walk naked (whom they call *naga*). While they are in the *kabak* none may call them forth whatsoever cause there be, because he hindereth the emperor's revenue.

The state became dependent on alcohol revenue. This meant that the state was dependent on the alcohol dependency of the population. Most countries have, to some extent or another, tried to limit their populations' drunkenness. They worry about crime and riots and sclerotic homes and broken livers. For the Russian state this has always been outweighed by the revenue. All of this leads us straight back to Nicholas II in 1914 choosing between sobriety and revenue, and, by breaking a 400-year-old tradition, bringing down a monarchy that was dependent on vodka.

There is nothing coincidental or accidental about the ubiquity of vodka.* Vodka has always been pushed over its milder rivals. The history of Russian drinking is the London gin craze in reverse: the terrible worry among the

---

* Vodka arrived in Russia in the fifteenth century. Despite some pretty stories, distillation was probably introduced by Genoese merchants on the Volga, and then you have the story of most spirits: a medicine that was taken so enthusiastically that it became a pleasure.

ruling classes that the people might sober up. The only two serious temperance campaigns in Russian history have been those of Mikhail Gorbachev and Nicholas Romanov.

Today, of course, all that has changed and Russia is in the grip of a new joyous sobriety and a gentle and caring government. The average Russian man consumes only half a bottle of vodka per day, and in 2010 the Finance Minister Aleksei Kudrin announced that the best way to solve the problems of public finance was to smoke more cigarettes and to drink much more vodka. "Those who drink," he proclaimed, "are giving more to help solve social problems such as boosting demographics, developing other social services and upholding birth rates."

CHAPTER 18

PROHIBITION

Prohibition in America worked jolly well, and don't let anyone tell you otherwise. When the 18th Amendment was repealed in 1933 after thirteen years in force, most of its supporters would have felt that it had worked a treat and done its job splendidly.

This may seem a rather eccentric diagnosis of what's commonly cited as the silliest law in history, but that's because the whole era has become so sodden with myth and mystique that even generally well-informed people tend to have a lot of misconceptions about what happened and why. The Popular Myth of Prohibition runs something like this:

1. Prohibition was introduced in 1920 by a small clique of conservative scrooges who didn't like alcohol. Nobody else wanted it.
2. The whole of the American population immediately went to a speakeasy in New York, where they drank twice as much as before and invented jazz.

3. This had the unforeseen consequence of leaving the USA in the hands of a man called Al Capone, who shot everyone with his tommy gun.

4. Eventually, in 1933, everybody decided that Prohibition had been silly, and the law was repealed.

5. The whole thing is a classic example of American Stupidity.

All of that is untrue, apart from the stuff about jazz, which was one of the surprise side effects of Prohibition, along with Italian cuisine and British passenger shipping. But we'll come to them. For the moment, let's take these point by point.

Who Wanted Prohibition?

The Prohibition movement wasn't conservative. It was feminist. It was also progressive, in something like the proper sense of the word: it was meant to help a nation reform and progress to a new and previously unheard-of state of sobriety. It was also Midwestern. Finally, the Prohibition movement was also—this one is the most surprising—not against alcohol.

It was against the saloon.

Long ago and far away, in Chapter 16, I mentioned that respectable women would never be found in a saloon. This raises the question of where they were, and the answer is that they were at home in high dudgeon, poverty and mortal fear. There was a popular perception throughout the West that husbands would get paid, go to the saloon, spend all their wages and return home penniless and angry, where they would beat their wives. The wives lived in bruised poverty, because the saloons took all the money.

Nobody knows to what extent this is true. Domestic violence is a notoriously difficult crime to get figures on while it's happening, and what precisely occurred in what percentage of log cabins is something that we shall never reconstruct. It must have happened a bit, and it may have happened a lot. What's important for our purposes is that people believed that this was what was happening. People wrote plays and novels about it. *Ten Nights in a Bar-Room and What I Saw There* was the second-best-selling American novel after *Uncle Tom's Cabin*, and both indirectly brought about amendments to the Constitution. The novel portrays the saloon as a villainous tempter that lures men in and forces them onto an inescapable path of alcoholism, violence, poverty and death punctuated only by the occasional appearance of a golden-haired daughter who begs Daddy to come home. But he *can't*; he's hooked. In *Ten Nights in a Bar-Room*, even the drinkers long for Prohibition.

The result was the great political awakening of the American female. Women at the time weren't meant to go into saloons or polling booths so they took to protesting in the streets outside the former. They would gather and kneel and pray. Nobody had seen anything like it.

In 1873 they formed the Woman's Christian Temperance Union. In the 1890s this gave way to the Anti-Saloon

League (ASL), which was dedicated to Prohibition. In both cases, the clue is firmly embedded in the name. But there is a much more subtle point. Though the rhetoric is hard to pick apart, they weren't really against alcohol. They were against a pattern of behavior associated with men in saloons. They absolutely did not care if a New York novelist had a glass of claret with her Sunday lunch. The thought had never crossed most of their minds. They were against the saloon, the saloon as instigator of domestic violence and domestic poverty.

It's significant that the ASL never required a personal pledge of abstinence from its members. Many of them, of course, were teetotalers, and there are an awful lot of speeches and pamphlets about the scourge of alcohol. But it is never clear whether alcohol means all alcohol or the alcohol drunk in saloons. And for many it meant the latter. There are three big groups in the forthcoming war. Drys were teetotalers who wanted Prohibition. Wets were drinkers who were against Prohibition. Drinking Drys were drinkers who thought other people shouldn't. They were a large voting bloc, and, as we shall see, their position wasn't quite as weird as it sounds.

There were others in the ASL—the usual mix of evangelicals, cranks and interested parties—but Prohibition as a movement was primarily feminist, progressive and Midwestern.

Then there's the question of when. Putting a date on Prohibition is nice and neat and easy and particularly easy in the days of the internet. It began on January 16, 1920, and ended on December 5, 1933. Except it didn't.

State laws prohibiting alcohol had been coming in for more than half a century. Maine was the first in 1851, although they found it unenforceable and repealed it a few years later. But as the nineteenth century waned and the new one waxed, state after state banned the good stuff. It reads like a list of the fallen. Kansas, 1880. Iowa, 1882. They weren't very effective as alcohol was easy to smuggle across state lines, but neither was Prohibition proper. By 1913 the majority of the American population lived under some form of state prohibition ban. The women were winning. And Germans were losing.

If the drive for Prohibition was run by Midwestern matrons, the drive against was run by Germans. They ran all the breweries. Like most immigrant groups the Germans simply had no tradition of teetotalism or temperance. They did have a tradition of making jolly good cold beer, and the beer earned them a lot of that money they spent on advertising campaigns for lager and against the Drys. These adverts portrayed beer as the health-giving German drink (as opposed to whiskey) drunk by happy German peasants and brewed to a traditional German recipe. Because everybody loved the Germans.

Then the First World War broke out. As usual with world wars, the Americans were a bit tardy, but when, in 1917, they finally worked out that World means World they joined in, noticed they needed to preserve their supplies of grain and so banned the distillation of spirits.

The pro-booze movement was now in a horrible position. Alcohol bans of various sorts were in place in most of the country. The movement against such bans was entirely identified with an enemy nation. And, horror of horrors and disaster of disasters, women were about to get the vote.

Drys had always been very effective voters as they were single issue. This meant that in any close-call election a candidate could guarantee himself a decisive bloc so long as he declared for Dry. This resulted in an awful lot of boozy politicians being publicly pro-Prohibition. With the imminent arrival of female suffrage, it was all over. Most of the women of America, many of the men of America, the Anti-Saloon League and every senator who wanted to keep his job supported the 18th Amendment without having any idea of what it meant.

The 18th Amendment, the one that is identified with Prohibition, the only amendment to curtail liberty, the only amendment to be repealed, never really says what it's banning. It just outlaws "intoxicating" drinks, without saying which ones they are.

Beer brewers were reasonably relaxed about the passing of the amendment. So were vintners. So were Drinking Drys. Everybody knew that Prohibition was not about alcohol, but about drunkenness, saloons and violence. It was about whiskey. Happy healthy wholesome beer was not intoxicating. It was extra-strength wine and spirits that were the problem. But Prohibition was in two parts: there was the constitutional amendment, and then there was the Volstead Act, which defined what that amendment actually meant. The Volstead Act defined "intoxicating" as over 0.5 percent ABV.

This was something of a surprise. Especially to the

Drinking Drys. The problem was that the ASL, like most pressure groups, had been hijacked by its most extreme members. They drafted the act and handed it to Andrew Volstead who presented it to Congress essentially unchanged.

The Ban

And it half worked. The greatest myth of Prohibition is that alcohol consumption actually increased. This is nonsense. Records of legal alcohol consumption end in 1920 and begin again in 1933, by which time they had fallen by just over half.

Alcohol consumption did increase in some places. New York is an obvious example. But this is where the myth of Prohibition and the proper history really diverge. We always hear about Prohibition in the big cities, because that's the exciting, glamorous, fun part of the story. Everybody was in speakeasies writing novels or massacring people on St. Valentine's Day while F. Scott Fitzgerald took notes and George Gershwin played piano in the corner.

This was not the case in rural Wyoming. The mobsters found that the population density presented a logistical nightmare in terms of delivery and HR. In small-town Midwest America, the place where Prohibition had started and from which its original advocates did their hailing, the saloons closed down.

In a small town there aren't enough back alleys to hide

from the police or to set up your speakeasy. Alcohol could get there, and did. People set up moonshine stills in the backwoods, and bootleggers would make occasional deliveries (it wasn't always the best stuff; in one incident in Wichita a dodgy batch of liquor permanently crippled 500 people in a single day). But, essentially, the saloon was closed, and with it the pattern of behavior was broken. Put bluntly, this is the point that the notoriously exciting Old West became the notoriously not exciting Midwest.

Unforeseen Consequences

In the cities Prohibition worked rather differently, but you could still just about argue that it worked. So I shall.

The definite downside was organized crime. This without doubt got something of a fillip from the good old 18th, though this can be overstated, and usually is. Under Al Capone's brutal regime of murder, Chicago's murder rate was at 10.4 bullet-ridden cadavers per 100,000 of population. In 2016 it was 27.9. The tommy-gun thing is wildly exaggerated in the popular imagination. Much worse was the corruption. Police forces, which were woefully underfunded, started taking bribes: a habit that they would find very hard to break even when Prohibition was long gone. In Boston there were four speakeasies on the same block as the police headquarters. In fact, the whole notion of abiding by the legal code took a bit of a bashing, and a new word was invented: "scofflaw" for somebody who laughed at the rules and spent his time in a speakeasy.

This is the moment that I should describe exactly what a speakeasy was like. But I can't. They were remarkably various. We may all have a firm idea based on films of a Judas window and a jazz band. But a speakeasy could just be somebody's apartment, and often was. A lot of rooming houses, for example, were owned by Italians. They would just open up a room where they served chianti and pasta. Historians of food cite this as the moment that Italian restaurants took off in America. People went for the wine and came back with a fondness for spaghetti.

People even went to black areas of town if they could find a drink there. In New York's main black newspaper a columnist observed that "the nightclubs have done more to improve race relations in ten years than the churches, white and black, have done in ten decades." The thing about the speakeasy is that it was a new form of drinking, invented from scratch, and so there were no rules. The saloon had been a place where a century of tradition had built up. A saloon had to have a brass rail and couldn't have women as customers. A speakeasy could do or be anything it wanted.

Probably the most surprising result of Prohibition was that women went to speakeasies. There was no rule or custom to prevent it. Now, if Prohibition's aim was to stop alcohol consumption, this was obviously a disaster. But if we see Prohibition as a means to break up the violent male world of the saloon, then this can be viewed as the greatest victory of all. The saloon had been a place "where a rattlesnake wouldn't take his mother." One speakeasy in New York put up a sign saying, "Through These Portals the Most Beautiful Girls in the World Pass OUT." Upmarket speakeasies even installed powder rooms. Victory was complete: women had the vote, and they had a cocktail to go with it.

Cocktails were very much the order of the day, and they were changed creatures. Just as in eighteenth-century London, the easiest bootleg liquor to make was bathtub gin. This was very low-quality stuff. A lot of it was made with stolen industrial alcohol and a lot of people got very ill. But even worse than the medical consequences was the taste. Cocktails had been around before in America (as we've seen), but they now changed in character, with the mixer there purely to mask the taste. Soda was no good as a mixer, but tonic water took off the sharp edge of bad gin. Whiskey, or what passed for it, was mixed with ginger beer until the taste was fully disguised. Coca-Cola had a massive sales boom, not as an alternative to alcohol, but as an accompaniment.

The biggest and longest-lasting effect that Prohibition had was that it destroyed the American drinks industry. Making good wine, whiskey, beer or anything else is a complicated business. It requires specialized equipment operated by specialist people. For thirteen years, in America, there were no legitimate breweries or distilleries. There were hoodlums mixing up rotgut in a bathtub, but anybody who had worked in the real, specialized, technical, complicated world of producing drinkable drinks was unemployed. They left the country. Or they retrained. There was no work for them. Even if they were willing to work for gangsters, gangsters didn't have the equipment or the supplies. You can't take a master distiller, give him some stolen industrial alcohol and a cellar and expect him to produce a fine malt whiskey with well-rounded flavors and notes of this and that. A sophisticated industry was wiped out. Whenever you see an advertisement for an American alcoholic drinks company that claims that they've been making their product the same way for 150 years, it's a lie.* There was a thirteen-year gap, during which all the old equipment was destroyed and all the people who knew the old method moved away and got other jobs.

Running alongside that was a decline in taste. A few people near the border or near a port could get hold of proper imported brands. But when repeal happened in 1933, most people hadn't even tasted proper booze in thirteen years. They couldn't remember what a good beer tasted like, which was convenient as the brewers couldn't remember how to make one. For the next half-century the USA had a well-deserved reputation for producing awful beer, rotten wine and revolting rye. This was the biggest and most baleful outcome of the 18th Amendment.

The final bizarre consequence of Prohibition was that the British sewed up the business of transatlantic passenger voyages, because their ships sold booze.†

* Oddly enough, the Jack Daniel's distillery in Lynchburg is in Moore County, which is still dry.

† Briefly, the USA tried to stop British boats docking in America with booze on board. This infuriated Parliament, which actually discussed the idea of refusing to allow American boats to dock in Britain *without* booze.

Why Did Prohibition End?

Prohibition did not end because people wanted a drink, it ended because people wanted jobs. The great crash of 1929 wrecked the American economy and they no longer had the luxury of banning businesses that could employ lots of destitute people (including passenger shipping). Anyhow, Prohibition had served its purpose. The saloon was gone.

George Ade, a resident of Chicago and a sodden and committed Wet, wrote a book in 1931 called *The Old Time Saloon: Not Wet—Not Dry, Just History*. At that time, he pointed out:

> More than half of the states were dry by legislative enact-ments twenty-five years ago. All of the public drinking places were restricted during the War Period and the Government measures wiping out every saloon on the map went into effect eleven years ago. Stop and count up. Even in the cities which are now regarded as Anti-Prohibition strongholds, no person under the age of thirty-two ever saw the inside of a saloon.

Ade, who was definitely pro-drink, admitted that the saloons were fundamentally awful and, though he wanted repeal of Prohibition, he conceded that public bars would never come back, because the saloon had been so funda-mentally male, malicious and soaked in whiskey.

The saloon never came back. Repeal legalized the

speakeasy; it legalized the restaurant that wanted to serve a glass of wine; it helped out the cruise-liner business, but it did not bring back the saloon. Prohibition had *worked*.

Obviously, there had been some in 1919 who were against alcohol per se, and who were disappointed by repeal. But they were the minority. Drys alone would never have forced through a change to the constitution. Prohibition was about a pattern of behavior associated with a particular kind of drinking establishment (hence the Drinking Drys), and that pattern of behavior was destroyed. Even if you want to see Prohibition as a campaign against alcohol (which it essentially wasn't), then it halved the alcohol intake of the USA. Consumption per capita didn't get up to pre-Prohibition levels until the 1970s. In 1939, some 42 percent of Americans didn't drink at all.

Finally, Prohibition didn't end in 1933. A lot of states remained dry. Prohibition didn't end until Mississippi finally repealed in 1966. One could argue that it's still going on as there are still dry counties.

America?

All non-Americans agree that America is stupid. For that matter, quite a lot of Americans agree that America is quite peculiarly stupid, like an embarrassing cousin at a family wedding. American stupidity is famous, and of a quite special kind. It's a unique sort of stupidity that allows them to put a chap on the moon (and bring him home afterward). It's the sort of idiocy that produces one-third of the Nobel Laureates in history. It is the dribbling imbecility that makes a country the richest and most powerful in the world economically, militarily, culturally and politically. American stupidity may often, in fact, look uncannily like American intelligence, but this cannot be the case because, if Americans weren't all chronically, extraordinarily, hadopelagically stupid, the rest of us would have nothing to feel smug about.

But we must confine ourselves to Prohibition and whether this idea, in and of itself, is an example of peculiarly American duncery. Careful readers of this book will know the answer from the previous chapter. The Russian vodka ban overlapped with Prohibition by five years. In Iceland a blanket alcohol ban was instituted in 1915; wines and spirits were legalized in 1935, beer in 1989. Finland had prohibition from 1919 till 1932. Norway banned spirits between 1917 and 1927. New Zealand held a referendum on prohibition in 1919 and the Drys won, until the votes were counted from the army who were overseas at the time. Still, it was a damned close-run thing.

Incidentally, many of the other bits and bobs that are meant to be peculiar to American Prohibition clearly weren't. Jazz music, though an American invention, caught on in countries like Britain where the speakeasy didn't exist. The flapper with her cocktail was just as much in evidence in London as in New York. There's quite as much booze in a novel by Evelyn Waugh as in one by Fitzgerald.

In fact, Alec Waugh, Evelyn's brother, claimed to have invented the cocktail party. He said that in the early 1920s in

England "There was nothing to do on winter evenings between half-past five and half-past seven." So he invited about thirty people around for tea at half-past five, and at quarter to six he brought out the daiquiris. Thus the cocktail party was invented by one chap on one day in London.

Except it probably wasn't. Trying to find the precise origins of a custom or a cocktail is the errand of a fool. The history is fog at the best of times, the history of drunkenness will never and can never be precisely recalled.

Evelyn Waugh had the right response to his brother: "His eyes widened and whitened in the way they did. 'I should be careful about making that boast in print.'"

Epilogue

In *Animal Farm*, the animals rise up in revolt because Mr. Jones the farmer is a drunk. At the end of the story they peer through the windows at the pigs, who are now drinking beer, and it is at that moment that they realize that the swine have become human.

This is the same story that was told in *The Epic of Gilgamesh* 4,000 years ago. Enkidu was a wild man who lived and ate and drank water with the animals. Then the priestess of Ishtar gives him beer, and the animals know that he is no longer one of them. In West Africa there's a story of how the creator god taught women how to make porridge and brew beer, and when they did it their fur and tails fell off and they became humans.

Wherever and whenever humans have lived they have gathered together to get intoxicated. The world experienced in sober solitude is not, and never has been, quite enough. The drugs vary of course, but they are always there.

Occasionally people talk of a "war on drugs," which is silly. Drugs are a constant. There is merely a war *between* drugs, and it is one that alcohol almost always wins. Mind you, if the government really did want to stamp out heroin or cocaine or whatnot, they could do it quite easily by removing the tax on booze. We are a simple species, and our choice of intoxicant is basically dependent on price and availability.

But what is drunkenness? What is this undying human ambition? There are so few constants to this constant. It's more that there are recurring characters. There's the strong man who can drink and drink and never get drunk—Socrates, Confucius and, to some extent, Stalin—but conversely there is the strong man who is drunk all the time—Peter the Great, Odin, Babur and, for that matter, Alexander the Great, who conquered the known world in something of a haze.

There is transitional drinking. We drink to move from one state to another. We drink to mark the end of the working day, or the end of the working week, or, if you are a member of the Suri tribe of Ethiopia, you drink to mark the beginning of the working day. As they put it: "Where there is no beer, there is no work." We drink at christenings, we drink at marriages, we drink at birthdays and we drink at funerals. And each time the drink means something; it means that an old state of affairs has gone, and that a new, slightly wobblier world is here. The Iteso of Kenya have a pleasant little ritual with new babies. A name is chosen, then the grandmother dips her finger in beer and puts it to the infant's mouth. If the baby sucks, then that is the name forever.

There is drinking as escape. The anthropologists' Third Place of the alehouse, the saloon or the *kabak*. But there are cultures where this is strikingly absent: Arabia, Persia or medieval England. Why don't we all drink at home? Why is the brass rail of the saloon or the pub fruit machine such a potent symbol of emancipation? From what are we escaping?

That we don't know the answer is, I think, the answer. Ever since mankind descended from the trees (with that useful mutation in ethanol-active Class IV alcohol dehydrogenases) we have asked ourselves two questions: "Is this all there is?" and "Do I have to?" Any society is an edifice of rules, and no matter how good those rules are, how reasonable, how just, how sensibly worked out for our own safety and welfare, we must occasionally escape them. Humankind has a compulsion to create rules and then to break them. This makes humankind a trifle silly, but also a trifle glorious.

The answer to the other question is similarly alcoholic. "Is this all there is?" Perhaps. Probably. But if we were given vastly more we would still be asking the same question. Humans are not satisfied, and that too is our glory. We're always looking for new oceans to cross, not because we need to, but because we're bored. We like to talk of the Ultimate Truth, but we would be so disappointed if we found it, because there would be no more. We long for a God we can't describe, because the only description we, as humans, can give is of a particularly crafty magician, and we know that God is more than that. God can never be *boring*. Humans are never bored when they're drunk.

William James still put it best: "Sobriety diminishes, discriminates, and says no; drunkenness expands, unites, and says yes."

Drunkenness is a heap of contradictions because it says yes to everything. Sometimes it is the instigator of violence and sometimes of peace. It makes us sing and it makes us sleep. To the Greeks it was a test of self-control, to the Norsemen it was the source of poetry, both good and bad. It's the joy of kings, and it's their downfall. It's the solace of the poor and the cause of their poverty. To governments it's the cause of the riots and a means of revenue. It's a proof of virility, a remover of virility, a means of seduction and a merry matron. Drunkenness is plague and a killer, a gift of the gods. It's the monk's necessity and the blood of the messiah. Drunkenness is a way of experiencing God and drunkenness is a god.

That's why it will always be around. Recently NASA published an internal report admitting that on at least two space-shuttle launches astronauts were properly, full-on, hiccup-and-happiness drunk. This does not surprise. People have been working drunk for millennia; and, to be honest, if I were about to be fired at several times the speed of sound toward an endless void, I would want a shot of the old reliable.

That's our past and that is, I'm sure, our future. Some-day, far from now, when the chimpanzees have taken over the breweries, when the elephants have occupied the distilleries and all the pubs are filled with lovelorn fruit flies, we shall, as a species, down our final earthly nog-gins, stumble into our spacecraft and leave behind this little ball of rock. It will be a great journey. As we break above the atmosphere leaving this old earth behind us, the gods will be there to cheer us on: Ninkasi, Hathor, Dionysus, Bacchus, Thor, the Centzon Totochtin, Madam Geneva. The Venus of Laussel will blow her horn, and get it the right way round for once. And we shall zoom, drunkenly, into the infinite.

And I know where we shall be heading: Sagittarius B2N. It's a cloud 26,000 light-years away, and those who start the journey will not be there for its completion. But it's 150 light-years across, and three million times the mass of the sun: an unimaginably vast cloud of naturally occurring space alcohol. And there, finally, in the nether reaches of nothingness we shall, because we are human, become cosmically drunk.

Bibliography

General

Iain Gately, *Drink: A Cultural History of Alcohol*, New York: Gotham, 2008

Tom Standage, *A History of the World in 6 Glasses*, New York: Anchor, 2005

Chapter 1: Evolution

Sarah Cains, Craig Blomeley, Mihaly Kollo, Romeo Rácz and Denis Burdakov, "Agrp Neuron Activity Is Required for Alcohol-Induced Overeating," *Nature Communications* 8: 14014 (2017), DOI: 10.1038/ncomms14014

Matthew A. Carrigan, Oleg Uryasev, Carole B. Frye, Blair L. Eckman, Candace R. Myers, Thomas D. Hurley and Steven A. Benner, "Hominids Adapted to Metabolize Ethanol Long Before Human-Directed Fermentation," *PNAS* 112:2 (2015), 458–63, DOI: 10.1073/pnas.1404167111

Charles Darwin, *The Descent of Man, and Selection in Relation to Sex*, 2 vols., London: John Murray, 1871

Robert Dudley, *The Drunken Monkey*, Berkeley: University of California Press, 2014

William J. A. Eiler II, Mario Džemidžić, K. Rose Case, Christina M. Soeurt, Cheryl L. H. Armstrong, Richard D. Mattes,

Sean J. O'Connor, Jaroslaw Harezlak, Anthony J. Acton, Robert V. Considine and David A. Kareken, "The Apéritif Effect: Alcohol's Effects on the Brain's Response to Food Aromas in Women," *Obesity* 23:7 (2015), 1386–93, DOI: 10.1002/oby.21109

The Works of Benjamin Franklin; Containing Several Political and Historical Tracts Not Included in Any Former Edition, and Many Letters, Official and Private, Not Hitherto Published; with Notes and a Life of the Author, ed. Jared Sparks, vol. 2, Boston: Tappan, Whittemore & Mason, 1836

A. P. Herbert, "Some Aspects of Hyperhydrophilia," in Cyril Ray (ed.), *The Compleat Imbiber*, vol. 1, London: Putnam, 1956

Sir John Lubbock, Bart., *The Beauties of Nature and the Wonders of the World We Live In*, London: Macmillan, 1892, pp. 62–63

Patrick E. McGovern, *Uncorking the Past*, Berkeley: University of California Press, 2009

Ronald K. Siegel, *Intoxication*, Rochester, Vermont: Park Street Press, 1989

Tom Standage, *A History of the World in 6 Glasses*, New York: Anchor, 2005

Chapter 2: The Prehistory of Drinking

Solomon H. Katz and Mary M. Voigt, "Bread and Beer: The Early Use of Cereals in the Human Diet," *Expedition* 28 (1986), 23–34, https://www.penn.museum/documents/publications/expedition/PDFs/28-2/Bread.pdf

Patrick E. McGovern, *Uncorking the Past*, Berkeley: University of California Press, 2009

"Symposium: Did Man Once Live by Beer Alone?," *American Anthropologist* 55:4 (1953), 515–26, http://onlinelibrary.wiley.com/doi/10.1525/aa.1953.55.4.02a00050/epdf

Chapter 3: Sumerian Bars

Lance Allred, "The Ancient Mesopotamian 'Tavern,'" AOS 2009

———, "Beer and Women in Mesopotamia," AOS 2008

J. A. Black, G. Cunningham, J. Ebeling, E. Flückiger-Hawker, E. Robson, J. Taylor and G. Zólyomi, *The Electronic Text Corpus of Sumerian Literature*, Oxford: Faculty of Oriental Studies, University of Oxford, 1998–2006, http://etcsl.orinst.ox.ac.uk/

Jerrold Cooper, "Prostitution," *Reallexikon der Assyriologie* 11 (2006), 12–22

Chapter 4: Ancient Egypt

Betsy M. Bryan, "Hatshepsut and Cultic Revelries in the New Kingdom," in José M. Galán, Besty M. Bryan and Peter F. Dorman (eds.), *Creativity and Innovation in the Reign of Hatshepsut*, SAOC 69, Chicago: The Oriental Institute, University of Chicago, 2014, pp. 93–123

John C. Darnell, "Hathor Returns to Medamûd," *Studien zur Altägyptischen Kultur* 22 (1995), 47–94

John C. Darnell, "The Rituals of Love in Ancient Egypt: Festival Songs of the Eighteenth Dynasty and the Ramesside Love Poetry," *Die Welt des Orients* 46 (2016), 22–61, DOI: 10.13109/wdor.2016.46.1.22

M. Depauw and M. Smith, "Visions of Ecstasy: Cultic Revelry before the Goddess Ai/Nehemanit. Ostraca Faculteit Letteren (K.U. Leuven) dem. 1–2," in F. Hoffmann and H. J. Thissen (eds.), *Res severa verum gaudium: Festschrift für Karl-Theodor Zauzich zum 65. Geburtstag am 8. Juni 2004, Studia Demotica* 6 (2004), 67–93

"Hymn from Ptolemaic Temple at Medamud," http://www.heth ert.org/hymnsprayers.htm#Hymn from Ptolemaic Temple at Medamud, 1999–2007 by Neferuhethert

William Kelly Simpson (ed.), *The Literature of Ancient Egypt: An Anthology of Stories, Instructions, and Poetry*, trans. R. O. Faulkner, Edward F. Wente, Jr., and William Kelly Simpson, New Haven: Yale University Press, 1972

William James, *The Varieties of Religious Experience*, London: Penguin Classics, 1985, p. 387

Chapter 5: The Greek Symposium

E. R. Dodds, *The Greeks and the Irrational*, Berkeley: University of California Press, 1951

Robin Osborne, "Intoxication and Sociality: The Symposium in the Ancient Greek World," in Phil Withington and Angela McShane (eds.), *Cultures of Intoxication, Past & Present*, Supplement 9, Oxford: Oxford University Press, 2014, 34–60

Chapter 6: Ancient Chinese Drinking

The Book of Songs [*Shih Ching*], trans. Arthur Waley, London: George Allen & Uwin, 1937

The Confucian Analects, trans. James Legge, Oxford: Clarendon Press, 1893

"The Shû King, the Religious Portions of the Shih King and the Hsiâo King," trans. James Legge, in *The Sacred Books of the East*, vol. 3, Oxford: Clarendon Press, 1879

Roel Sterckx, "Alcohol and Historiography in Early China," *Global Food History*, 1:1 (2015), 13–32

———, *Food, Sacrifice, and Sagehood in Early China*, Cambridge: Cambridge University Press, 2011

Chapter 7: The Bible

Robert Alter, *The Five Books of Moses: A Translation with Commentary*, New York: Norton, 2004

———, *The Wisdom Books: Job, Proverbs, and Ecclesiastes. A Translation with Commentary*, New York: Norton, 2010

C. K. Barrett, *The Gospel According to St John*, 2nd ed., London: SPCK, 1978

Campbell Bonner, "A Dionysiac Miracle at Corinth," *American Journal of Archaeology* 33:3 (July–Sept. 1929), 368–75

Barnabas Lindars, *The Gospel of John*, The New Century Bible Commentary, London: Marshall, Morgan & Scott, 1972

Chapter 8: The Roman Convivium

Susan E. Alcock, "Power Lunches in the Eastern Roman Empire," *Michigan Quarterly Review* 42:4 (2003), 591–606, https://quod.lib.umich.edu/cgi/t/text/text-idx?cc=mqr;c=mqr;c=mqrarchive;idno=act2080.0042.401;rgn=main;view=text;xc=1;g=mqrg

W. A. Becker, *Gallus: or Roman Scenes of the Time of Augustus*, trans. Rev. Frederick Metcalfe, London: Longmans, Green, 1886

Chapter 9: The Dark Ages

Alcuin of York, "Letter to Higbald," in Stephen Allott, *Alcuin of York*, York: William Sessions, 1974; reprinted in Paul Edward Dutton (ed.), *Carolingian Civilization: A Reader*, Peterborough, Ontario: Broadview Press, 1993, pp. 123–25

Histories of the Kings of Britain, by Geoffrey of Monmouth, trans. Sebastian Evans, London: Dent, 1904

Priscus, "Dining with Attila," trans. in J. H. Robinson, *Readings in European History*, vol. 1, Boston: Ginn, 1904

St. Benedict's Rule for Monasteries, trans. from the Latin by Leonard J. Doyle, Collegeville, Minnesota: The Liturgical Press, 1948

Tacitus, *Germany and Its Tribes*, in Alfred John Church and William Jackson Brodribb (eds.), *Complete Works of Tacitus*, New York: Random House, 1942; edited for Perseus by Lisa Cerrato, http://www.perseus.tufts.edu/hopper/text?doc=Perseus:abo:phi,1351,002:22

Chapter 10: Drinking in the Middle East

Shahab Ahmed, *What Is Islam? The Importance of Being Islamic*, Princeton: Princeton University Press, 2016

Elena Andreeva, *Russia and Iran in the Great Game: Travelogues and Orientalism*, London: Routledge, 2007

Franciscus de Billerbeg, *Most rare and straunge discourses, of Amurathe the Turkish emperor that now is with the warres betweene him and the Persians: the Turkish triumph, lately had at Constantinople*, London, 1584

James B. Fraser, *Narrative of a journey into Khorasān, in the years 1821 and 1822. Including some account of the countries to the north-east of Persia; with remarks upon the national character, government, and resources of that kingdom*, London: Longman, Hurst, Rees, Orme, Brown & Green, 1825

"Illegal Alcohol Booming in Iran," BBC News, Sept. 15, 2011, http://www.bbc.co.uk/news/world-middle-east-14939866

Kai Kā'ūs ibn Iskandar, Prince of Gurgān, *A Mirror for Princes: The Qābūs nūma*, trans. from the Persian by Reuben Levy, London: Cresset Press, 1951

Philip F. Kennedy, *The Wine Song in Classical Arabic Poetry*, Oxford: Clarendon Press, 1997

Rudi Matthee, "Alcohol in the Islamic Middle East: Ambivalence and Ambiguity," in Phil Withington and Angela McShane (eds.), *Cultures of Intoxication, Past & Present*, Supplement 9, Oxford: Oxford University Press, 2014, 100–25

Poems of Wine and Revelry: The Khamriyyat of Abu Nuwas, trans. Jim Colville, London: Kegan Paul, 2005

Chapter 11: The *Viking* Sumbl

The Poetic Edda, trans. from the Icelandic by Henry Adams Bellows, Princeton: Princeton University Press, 1936, http://www.sacred-texts.com/neu/poe/poe.pdf

Joshua Rood, "Drinking with Óðinn: Alcohol and Religion in Heathen Scandinavia," Reykjavik: Háskóli Íslands, 2014, http://www.academia.edu/8640034/Drinking_with_%C3%93%C3%B0inn_Alcohol_and_Religion_in_Heathen_Scandinavia

Snorri Sturluson, *The Prose Edda*, trans. Jesse L. Byock, London: Penguin Classics, 2005

Chapter 12: The Medieval Alehouse

Martha Carlin, "The Host," in Stephen H. Rigby (ed.), *Historians on Chaucer: The "General Prologue" to the Canterbury Tales*, Oxford: Oxford University Press, 2014, pp. 460–80 (updated version kindly supplied by the author)

———, *Medieval Southwark*, London: The Hambledon Press, 1986

Peter Clark, *The English Alehouse: A Social History 1200–1830*, London: Longman, 1983

Chapter 13: The Aztecs

Rebecca Earle, "Indians and Drunkenness in Spanish America," in Phil Withington and Angela McShane (eds.), *Cultures of Intoxication, Past & Present*, Supplement 9, Oxford: Oxford University Press, 2014, 81–99

Munro S. Edmonson (ed.), *Sixteenth-Century Mexico: The Work of Sahagún*, Albuquerque: University of New Mexico Press, 1974

Jacques Soustelle, *Daily Life of the Aztecs on the Eve of the Spanish Conquest*, trans. Patrick O'Brian, London: Weidenfeld & Nicolson, 1961

Chapter 14: The Gin Craze

Patrick Dillon, *Gin: The Much Lamented Death of Madam Geneva*, London: Thistle, 2013

Bernard Mandeville, *An enquiry into the causes of the frequent executions at Tyburn: and a proposal for some regulations concerning felons in prison, and the good effects to be expected from them*, London: Roberts, 1725

The Political State of Great Britain, vol. 51, London: T. Cooper, 1736, pp. 350–51

Dudley Bradstreet, *The life and uncommon adventures of Captain Dudley Bradstreet*, Dublin: Powell, 1755

Jessica Warner, *Craze: Gin and Debauchery in an Age of Reason*, London: Profile, 2003

Chapter 15: Australia

Matthew Allen, "The Temperance Shift: Drunkenness, Responsibility and the Regulation of Alcohol in NSW, 1788–1856," PhD thesis, University of Sydney, 2013

Alan Atkinson, *The Europeans in Australia: A History*, vol. 1, Oxford: Oxford University Press, 1997

Governor Phillip's Instructions, April 25, 1787, http://www .foundingdocs.gov.au/resources/transcripts/nsw2_doc_1787 .pdf

Tom Gilling, *Grog: A Bottled History of Australia's First 30 Years*, Sydney, NSW: Hachette Australia, 2016

David Hunt, *Girt: The Unauthorised History of Australia*, vol. 1, Collingwood, Victoria: Black, 2013

Henry Jeffreys, *Empire of Booze*, London: Unbound, 2016

Watkin Tench, *A Narrative of the Expedition to Botany-Bay*, London: Debrett, 1789, http://adc.library.usyd.edu.au/data-2/ p00039.pdf

Chapter 16: The Wild West Saloon

George Ade, *The Old Time Saloon: Not Wet—Not Dry, Just History*, Chicago: University of Chicago Press, 2016

Susan Cheever, *Drinking in America*, London: Hachette, 2016

Dan De Quille, *History of the Big Bonanza: An Authentic Account of the Discovery, History and Working of the World Renowned Comstock Silver Lode of Nevada*, Hartford, Connecticut: American Publishing, 1876

El Paso *Daily Times*, June 2, 1884

Richard Erdoes, *Saloons of the Old West*, New York: Knopf, 1979

Pierre Lacour, *The manufacture of liquors, wines, and cordials, without the aid of distillation. Also the manufacture of effervescing beverages and syrups, vinegar, and bitters. Prepared and arranged expressly for the trade*, New York: Dick & Fitzgerald, 1853

Randolph Roth, "Homicide Rates in the American West," Ohio State University, Criminal Justice Research Center, 2010, https:// cjrc.osu.edu/research/interdisciplinary/hvd/homicide-rates-american-west

Christine Sismondo, *America Walks into a Bar*, Oxford: Oxford University Press, 2011

Chapter 17: Russia

Sir John Barrow, *A Memoir of the Life of Peter the Great*, London, 1839

David Christian, *"Living Water": Vodka and Russian Society on the Eve of Emancipation*, New York: Oxford University Press, 1990

Giles Fletcher, *Of the Russe Common Wealth*, London, 1591 (reprinted in *Russia at the Close of the Sixteenth Century . . .* , ed. Edward A. Bond, London: Hakluyt Society, 1856)

Mark Lawrence Schrad, "Moscow's Drinking Problem," *New York Times*, April 16, 2011

Mark Lawrence Schrad, *Vodka Politics: Alcohol, Autocracy, and the Secret History of the Russian State*, Oxford: Oxford University Press, 2014

Chapter 18: Prohibition

George Ade, *The Old Time Saloon: Not Wet—Not Dry, Just History*, Chicago: University of Chicago Press, 2016

Jack S. Blocker, Jr. "Did Prohibition Really Work? Alcohol Prohibition as a Public Health Innovation," *American Journal of Public Health* 96:2 (Feb. 2006), 233–43, http://ajph.aphapub lications.org/doi/full/10.2105/AJPH.2005.065409

Daniel Okrent, *Last Call: The Rise and Fall of Prohibition*, New York: Scribner, 2010

Acknowledgments

This book would have been impossible to write without the kind help of many people who took the time to meet me or to reply to my impertinent questions. I owe a debt of gratitude to Professor Patrick McGovern, Professor Paul Strohm, Professor Judith Jesch, Professor John C. Darnell, Professor Betsy Bryan, Professor Roland Mayer (with thanks for his notes on Roman vomiting), Dr. Lance B. Allred, Professor Martha Carlin, Professor Faramerz Dabhoiwala, David Langford, Dr. Sam Gilbert, Tom O'Shea, Ian Irvine, Elena Cook, Hilary Scott, Derek Robinson and Stephen Ryan. Any facts that have somehow infiltrated this book are down to them; all mistakes, absurdities, inconsistencies and the drawing of wild conclusions are entirely down to me.

Moreover, for reading through drafts and making helpful suggestions about Oxford commas, I should thank my parents, John Goldsmith and Jane Seeber.

Index

About the Author

Born in London in 1977, **Mark Forsyth** (aka The Inky Fool) was given a copy of the *Oxford English Dictionary* as a christening present and has never looked back. His book *The Etymologicon* was a *Sunday Times* number one bestseller, and his TED Talk "What's a Snollygoster?" has had more than half a million views. He has also written a specially commissioned essay, "The Unknown Unknown," for Independent Booksellers Week and the introduction for the new edition of the *Collins English Dictionary*. He lives in London with his dictionaries, and blogs at blog.inkyfool.com.